A FUTURE
AND A HOPE

ENCOURAGEMENT FOR SINGLE WOMEN

JANAN TERPSTRA

Copyright © 2019 Janan Terpstra
All rights reserved.

No part of this book may be reproduced in any manner without the written consent of the publisher except for brief excerpts in critical reviews or articles.

All quoted Scripture is from the New Living Version unless otherwise noted. Complete passages that are referenced can be found in the appendix.

ISBN: 978-1-61244-723-0
Library of Congress Control Number: 2019903275

Printed in the United States of America

Halo Publishing International
1100 NW Loop 410
Suite 700 - 176
San Antonio, Texas 78213
www.halopublishing.com
contact@halopublishing.com

Dedicated to my single sisters in Christ who are holding Jesus to His Word

"'For I know the plans I have for you,' says the LORD. 'They are plans for good and not for disaster, to give you a future and a hope.'"

-Jeremiah 29:11

Acknowledgments

Being alone for so long taught me to deeply value my husband. Thank you, Bob, for encouraging me every day to continue writing this book. I also want to thank the pastors on my journey who helped to color my understanding of Christ: Richard Dresselhaus, Rick Petersen (deceased) and Ed Chapman (San Diego, CA), Mark Jobe (Chicago, IL), Randy Simonson (Hudson, WI). And last but not least, I am grateful to my long-time friend Lynn Stafford who read this manuscript in its early stages and whose wise input I value.

Contents

Prologue	9
Why Did This Have to Happen?	11
Postponement	18
Something New	24
And Then the Angel Left	30
Fat Babies	36
Stagnant	42
Fear	48
Fear Part 2	57
Focus on the True God	64
Out of Focus	70
Prayer Misconceptions	75
Bouncy House Prayers	83
Prayer Hindrances	89
Doubt	95
Intercession	102
Unanswered Prayer	110
Pity Party	117
Perseverance	124
Perseverance Part 2	130

Perseverance Part 3	136
Complete the Work	144
Burn Out	152
Burn Out, Part 2	159
Voice of god	166
Hard-hearted	171
Perfect Woman	180
Enlarged Territory	190
Enemies of Our Mind	200
God Takes Action	208
Poor Choices	213
Jealousy/Envy	220
Running Away	227
Fully Known	232
He Delights in You	240
Standing Firm	247
Failure is a Fact of Life	255
Go Home!	261
I Will Make You My Wife Forever	269
Bibliography	276
Appendix	279
My story	280
My Father's Voice	284

Prologue

I was sitting in the sunshine on a patio outside of a recording studio in Nashville, TN. Along with a team of friends, my husband and I had pooled our efforts to bring our buddy Joe Loftus to the city of music to make a cd. I was enjoying a moment of quiet, reflecting on the blessings in my life and how far I had come. At that moment, I felt an urge from the Holy Spirit to write down my journey. Many years later, this book is the culmination of what began with that nudge from God.

I was 46 when I got married for the first and only time. I was 17 when I encountered the radical person of Jesus in a way that made me sit up and take notice. So, for nearly 30 years, I was a single woman in a community of believers, of varying denominations, who did not quite know what to do with me. Although I served in leadership most of that time, my inability to find a spouse perplexed and bothered most of my church family.

This book is dedicated to all the single women out there who are faithfully following Christ, who *want* to get married but who are honestly enjoying life and serving wholeheartedly without a man. I salute you and pray from the depths of my soul that my experiences and, more importantly, the Scriptures in these pages will encourage and challenge you to live for Jesus.

> "MY EYES ARE STRAINING TO SEE YOUR PROMISES COME TRUE. WHEN WILL YOU COMFORT ME?"
>
> - PSALM 119:82

Many times I have bought an inspirational book to find it on the table by my recliner weeks later. At that moment, I say, "Oh, yeah, God. Um. . . sorry about that. I meant to be good!" Don't let Satan interfere. Read at your own pace. There are a lot of interactive questions, so you may consider journaling or, even better, reading with a friend or a small group.

May you be one of the ones He finds on His search.

> "THE EYES OF THE LORD SEARCH THE WHOLE EARTH IN ORDER TO STRENGTHEN THOSE WHOSE HEARTS ARE FULLY COMMITTED TO HIM."
>
> - 2 CHRONICLES 16:9

1
Why Did This Have to Happen?

"Faith does not eliminate questions.
But faith knows where to take them."

-Elisabeth Elliot

"Why am I still single? Doesn't God love me?" I must have asked that question a thousand times. I would think that the reason I wasn't married was that I was overweight. Then, I would receive a wedding invitation from a friend who was much heavier than me. Naturally, I assumed I was just flawed. I could work on losing weight, but how could I change my whole personality? Had I really offended the Lord to the point that I was to be punished indefinitely?

Maybe you can relate to these crazy thoughts that were bouncing around in my head. Maybe you have a different issue. But I'm sure that every one of us has been through a tough time, whether it was a life-altering tragedy or just a rough patch.

I did finally get married at the age of 46 to Bob. He had his own reasons to constantly ask God "Why?" Before I met him, Bob had been severely injured, and, barring a miracle, he will spend the rest of his life in a wheelchair. After multiple discussions and searching Scripture many times, we have decided that this is a question the Lord does not answer. Think of Job, a man who demanded answers. God lists all His credentials and ends up saying:

Job 40:1-2

Do you still want to argue with the Almighty?
You are God's critic, but do you have the answers?

To which Job, very wisely, replies:

Job 40:4-5

⁴"I am nothing—how could I ever find the answers?
I will cover my mouth with my hand.
⁵ I have said too much already.
I have nothing more to say."

Sometimes, I think the Lord does reveal His design to build our faith, but other times He pushes us to trust without knowing the answers. After all, we "do not know the Lord's thoughts or understand his plan" (Micah 4:12a).

Trying to figure out God can be dangerous. Remember the story of Joseph and all that he endured. When he became the head honcho of Potiphar's house, he may have thought, "Ah, *this* is why God allowed my brothers to sell me into slavery." If so, his faith would have soured soon after he was thrown in jail for a trumped-up rape charge.[1] But God's end game was for Joseph to become second in command of all Egypt. As Joseph tells his brothers at the end of the story:

Genesis 50:20

You intended to harm me, but God intended it all for good. He brought me to this position so I could save the lives of many people.

Sometimes God will reveal answers, but we have to be willing to wait patiently.

James 1:2-4

Dear brothers and sisters, when troubles of any kind come your way, consider it an opportunity for great joy. For you know that when your faith is tested, your endurance has a chance to grow. So let it grow, for when your endurance is fully developed, you will be perfect and complete, needing nothing.

After all, it took over ten years for David to gain the throne. Paul was called on the road to Damascus, but it was at least ten more years before he went on his first missionary trip.[2] God wants you for the long haul. His goal is to perfect you, which is unlikely to happen overnight.

The relationship I had with the boyfriend before meeting my husband was disastrous. In hindsight, however, if I hadn't been treated badly by him, I would never have been ready for Bob. *Thank you, Lord, for not giving me what I was asking for at that time.* I often think of Garth Brooks' wonderful song lyrics: "Sometimes God's greatest gifts are unanswered prayers." I still thought Bob was a little too ordinary, boring, and sweet, rather than the charismatic, razzmatazz man I thought I needed. But because

I'd been burned (and because my dad gave me great advice), I gave "Mr. Nice Guy" a chance.

I've been through a lot of heartaches and haven't yet figured out the whys and wherefores of my experiences. God does warn us, after all:

<ins>Isaiah 55:8-9</ins>

> My thoughts are nothing like your thoughts. . . and my ways are far beyond anything you could imagine. For just as the heavens are higher than the earth, so my ways are higher than your ways and my thoughts higher than your thoughts.

Madeleine Engle's poem "Act III, Scene ii" describes what we often feel in life, and I encourage you to find this poem online.[3]

A time in my life that still hurts deeply is when my best girlfriend said she never wanted to see me again. Although I believe I have forgiven her, it doesn't erase this pain. We had been roomies, and I helped her raise her two children; losing all three relationships overnight was devastating. I've never been divorced, thank the Lord, but that's what I compare it to emotionally. I won't go into the details, and I undoubtedly contributed to her anger against me. The point is that I have to deal with my past without understanding why it happened. I do believe that God wants to transform our pain into something good. I heard the testimony of a missionary couple who had lost their newborn baby. He said he doesn't understand God's hand, but he still trusts His heart. That is a great place to be.

We will never trust God's heart if we constantly rehearse the past in our minds or retell the story over and over again to friends or family.

<ins>Hebrews 12:15</ins>

> Look after each other so that none of you fails to receive the grace of God. Watch out that no poisonous root of bitterness grows up to trouble you, corrupting many.

One way to detect this dangerous root is hearing yourself say, "I'm never going to let that happen again." There is a fine line between learning the lesson of who to trust and hardening your heart so much that it isn't open to love. When looking back, remember to "Be thankful in all circumstances, for this is God's will for you who belong to Christ Jesus" (1 Thessalonians 5:8).

Remember that your suffering makes God weep, like when Jesus cried at Lazarus' tomb. Exodus 3:7 says that "He hears your cries of distress."

Isaiah 63:9

In all their suffering he also suffered, and he personally rescued them. In his love and mercy he redeemed them. He lifted them up and carried them through all the years.

Do you not know how to pray when you are feeling miserable and ornery and confused? Try using David's prayer:

Psalm 86:1-7

[1] Bend down, O Lord, and hear my prayer;
answer me, for I need your help.

[2] Protect me, for I am devoted to you.
Save me, for I serve you and trust you.
You are my God.

[3] Be merciful to me, O Lord,
for I am calling on you constantly.

[4] Give me happiness, O Lord,
for I give myself to you.

[5] O Lord, you are so good, so ready to forgive,
so full of unfailing love for all who ask for your help.

[6] Listen closely to my prayer, O Lord;
hear my urgent cry.

[7] I will call to you whenever I'm in trouble,
and you will answer me.

The Lord doesn't orchestrate circumstances like a puppet master, but He is in the midst of everything, ready to bring comfort or wisdom or strength. And He can do that because He lived on earth as a human and He knows from first-hand experience what you are going through. My feelings of betrayal over my friend dumping me was a poor reflection of what Jesus must have endured the moment Judas kissed Him in the garden.

Hebrews 2:18

Since he himself has gone through suffering and testing, he is able to help us when we are being tested.

POINTS TO PONDER:

Which of the Scriptures cited above resonated the most in your heart?

_____

Copy that verse in your prayer journal. If you don't keep a journal begin a new notebook now or write it on the line above.

PRAYER:

Lord Jesus, I know You understand my frustration and You realize I have unanswered questions about the pain in my life. Help me to trust Your love for me even when I don't see the evidence I think I need.

2
Postponement

"Begin to weave and God will give you the thread."

–German Proverb

It's easy to get frustrated when what we want to happen seems to be unimportant to God. We need to understand that He may be postponing your blessing or answer, which is very different than not caring. I must admit that this is not the wisdom most of us want to hear. I remember meeting a missionary who didn't get married until she was over 60, and I was terrified. I thought, "No, God, don't make that *my* testimony!"

What are you waiting for in your life? Is it marriage or children or a better job or more money? I bet you'll be able to relate to a little shepherdess called Much-Afraid. *Hinds Feet on High Places* by Hannah Hurnard is a Christian classic. The story is an allegory about Much-Afraid following the Shepherd (Jesus) to the High Places (or, a deeper walk with Christ).

> "Shepherd," she said despairingly, "I can't understand this. The guides you gave me say that we must go down there into that desert, turning right away from the High Places altogether. You don't mean that, do you? You can't contradict yourself. Tell them that we are not to go there and show us another way...."
>
> He looked at her and answered very gently, "That is the path, Much-Afraid, and you are to go down there"
>
> "Oh no," she cried. "You can't mean it. You said if I would trust you, you would bring me to the High Places, and that path leads right away from them. It contradicts all that you promised."
>
> "No," said the Shepherd, "it is not contradiction, only postponement for the best to become possible....
>
> Much-Afraid, do you love me enough to accept the postponement and the apparent contradiction of the promise, and to go down there with me into the desert?"...
>
> "I do love you, you know that I love you. Oh forgive me because I can't help my tears. I will go down with you into the wilderness, right away from the promise, if you really wish it. Even if you cannot tell me why it has to be, I will

go with you, for you know I do love you and you have the right to choose for me anything that you please."[4]

Ultimately, God is God and we are not. I think a part of us secretly hates that fact. He has every right to do what He wants in your life because a) He is perfect and b) He loves you unconditionally.

Romans 9:20-22

Who are you, a mere human being, to argue with God? Should the thing that was created say to the one who created it, 'Why have you made me like this?' [21] When a potter makes jars out of clay, doesn't he have a right to use the same lump of clay to make one jar for decoration and another to throw garbage into? [22] In the same way, even though God has the right to show his anger and his power, he is very patient with those on whom his anger falls, who are destined for destruction.

Isaiah 29:16

How foolish can you be?
He is the Potter, and he is certainly greater than you, the clay!
Should the created thing say of the one who made it,
'He didn't make me'?
Does a jar ever say,
'The potter who made me is stupid'?

Have you ever had a car that leaked oil? I did and I remember having to constantly use the dipstick to see what my levels were like that day. Here's a little exercise to check your trust level.

Take a blank sheet of paper and write the following:

Dear Father God,
I will. . .

Love,
(Your Name)

Then tell God that He is free to fill in the blank. If you are thinking "How can I agree to something before I know what it is?" then you are not trusting that *everything* God has in store for your future is for your good.

I lived in San Diego for 20 years and served as co-leader for a singles' group at my church. I got my graduate degree in theology and decided to put it to good use as a missionary. I then served in an inner-city fellowship in Chicago for four years.

At one point in my fundraising to be a missionary, I caught myself secretly hoping the money wouldn't come through. Then I would have an easy excuse. I would have the reputation of being "spiritual" and "brave" but wouldn't actually have to walk in trust. Of course, that didn't happen. The years in Chicago were difficult in many ways, but the things God taught me about Himself were priceless.

And, of course, to be honest, sometimes the hard things we go through can be a form of communication. C.S. Lewis points out that "God whispers to us in our pleasures, speaks to us in our conscience, but shouts in our pains; it is his megaphone to rouse a deaf world."[5]

Bob and I were on a road trip when we got a very unexpected call from my stepfather. My mom had suffered from Parkinson's disease for years but was not "terminal" in the near future. She died from choking on a hot dog. We were in El Paso, TX at the time. The next day was Sunday. We could either start driving east to Missouri for the funeral or follow our original plan to take a day off and go to church. I knew that if there was ever a time I needed to sit in God's presence and worship, this was the time. We went to a mega church and heard a great message that was given "just for me." Don't you love it when hundreds of people are listening, but you know the secret? In those moments, you know that God is speaking to *your* heart.

The preacher shared the story of Jesus showing up unexpectedly to visit the disciples after the resurrection.

John 21:1-9

[1] Later, Jesus appeared again to the disciples beside the Sea of Galilee. This is how it happened. [2] Several of the disciples were there—Simon Peter, Thomas (nicknamed the Twin), Nathanael from Cana in Galilee, the sons of Zebedee, and two other disciples.

[3] Simon Peter said, "I'm going fishing."

"We'll come, too," they all said. So they went out in the boat, but they caught nothing all night.

⁴ At dawn Jesus was standing on the beach, but the disciples couldn't see who he was. ⁵ He called out, "Fellows, have you caught any fish?"

"No," they replied.

⁶ Then he said, "Throw out your net on the right-hand side of the boat, and you'll get some!" So they did, and they couldn't haul in the net because there were so many fish in it.

⁷ Then the disciple Jesus loved said to Peter, "It's the Lord!" When Simon Peter heard that it was the Lord, he put on his tunic (for he had stripped for work), jumped into the water, and headed to shore. ⁸ The others stayed with the boat and pulled the loaded net to the shore, for they were only about a hundred yards from shore. ⁹ When they got there, they found breakfast waiting for them—fish cooking over a charcoal fire, and some bread.

I'm sure there are many excellent points from this passage, but the one that sticks with me is Peter's response to seeing Jesus. He could have easily waited until the boat headed to shore. The other disciples were probably eager to see their Lord and friend too. But Peter jumped into the water. He was that desperate to see Jesus. It was the attitude of "I don't have five minutes. I need Jesus *right now.*" That's how I felt with the loss of my mom like a dagger in my side. I needed the comfort only He could give. Did I get the answers to my questions? Not one. But I did get love and hope and companionship.

POINTS TO PONDER:

Fill in the blank.

Lord, I feel like Much-Afraid, scared that You will postpone my desire to _____ and afraid to trust Your timing.

PRAYER:

Father God help me to put aside my agenda for my life and to desire You. Give me such a desperate hunger for Your friendship that I am ready to swim to shore to be with You even if You don't give me the answers I seek right away.

3
Something New

"We are products of our past, but we don't have to be prisoners of it."

-Rick Warren

It can be so tempting to live in the past. We don't even realize that's what we are doing, but every time we bring up the way we have been mistreated or the horrible things that happened to us, we are refusing to let go and move forward. Sometimes, we hold on to a broken relationship or a missed opportunity. We must trust that God is not surprised by what happened and that He still has great things in store.

Once, I listened to a retreat speaker ask a room full of women: "Would you pack up your trash can from home and carry it around with you?" No one else wants to see our garbage. There is a time to reveal it and be healed, but we often have the power to put it down and walk away. We need to learn how to distance ourselves from the broken record of what went wrong and move on to a glorious future with Jesus.

I had a hard time letting go of feelings of betrayal from various breakups. Are you holding on to the past? Read the following verses slowly. Then, write down a principle that will help you walk into the amazing future that God has for you.

Isaiah 43:17-19

[18] "But forget all that—
it is nothing compared to what I am going to do.
[19] For I am about to do something new.
See, I have already begun! Do you not see it?
I will make a pathway through the wilderness.
I will create rivers in the dry wasteland.

Principle: _____

_____

Philippians 3:12-14

[12] I don't mean to say that I have already achieved these things or that I have already reached perfection. But I press on to possess that perfection for which Christ Jesus first possessed me. [13] No, dear brothers and sisters, I have not achieved it, but I focus on this one thing: Forgetting the

past and looking forward to what lies ahead, ¹⁴ I press on to reach the end of the race and receive the heavenly prize for which God, through Christ Jesus, is calling us.

Principle: _____

_____

Luke 9:61-62

⁶¹ Another said, "Yes, Lord, I will follow you, but first let me say good-bye to my family."

⁶² But Jesus told him, "Anyone who puts a hand to the plow and then looks back is not fit for the Kingdom of God.

Principle: _____

_____

Exodus 16:11-21

Then the Lord said to Moses,¹² "I have heard the Israelites' complaints. Now tell them, 'In the evening you will have meat to eat, and in the morning you will have all the bread you want. Then you will know that I am the Lord your God.'"

¹³ That evening vast numbers of quail flew in and covered the camp. And the next morning the area around the camp was wet with dew. ¹⁴ When the dew evaporated, a flaky substance as fine as frost blanketed the ground. ¹⁵ The Israelites were puzzled when they saw it. "What is it?" they asked each other. They had no idea what it was.

And Moses told them, "It is the food the Lord has given you to eat.¹⁶ These are the Lord's instructions: Each household should gather as much as it needs. Pick up two quarts for each person in your tent."

¹⁷ So the people of Israel did as they were told. Some gathered a lot, some only a little. ¹⁸ But when they measured it out, everyone had just enough. Those who gathered a lot had nothing left over, and those who gathered only a little had enough. Each family had just what it needed.

¹⁹ Then Moses told them, "Do not keep any of it until morning." ²⁰ But some of them didn't listen and kept some of it until morning. But by then it was full of maggots and had a terrible smell. Moses was very angry with them.

²¹ After this the people gathered the food morning by morning, each family according to its need. And as the sun became hot, the flakes they had not picked up melted and disappeared.

Principle: _____

_____

Genesis 19:23-26

Lot reached the village just as the sun was rising over the horizon.²⁴ Then the Lord rained down fire and burning sulfur from the sky on Sodom and Gomorrah. ²⁵ He utterly destroyed them, along with the other cities and villages of the plain, wiping out all the people and every bit of vegetation.²⁶ But Lot's wife looked back as she was following behind him, and she turned into a pillar of salt.

Principle: _____

_____

Jeremiah 29:11

"For I know the plans I have for you," says the Lord. "They are plans for good and not for disaster, to give you a future and a hope."

Principle: _____

_____

After you have meditated on the above, LET THE PAST GO. Pay close attention to what Sproul has to say:

> What do you do with the person who says, "I've asked God to forgive me about this, but I still feel guilty"? I hear that statement over and over again. I usually say to these people, "If you still feel guilty, then pray to God again. But this time

don't ask Him to forgive you for the sin that is haunting you. Rather, ask Him to forgive you for insulting His integrity by refusing to accept His forgiveness. Who are you to refuse to forgive yourself when God has forgiven you? When God promises to forgive His people when they repent, He is not playing games. If He says He will forgive you, then He will forgive you. And if God forgives you, you are forgiven."[6]

POINTS TO PONDER:

Name something from your past that you would like to leave behind.

_____

Which Scripture from this chapter gave you the most encouragement?

_____

PRAYER:

Holy God, please reveal to me any garbage from my past that I am still hauling around. Give me the strength to let You toss my trash.

_____

4
And Then the Angel Left

"The Bible recognizes no faith that does not lead to obedience, nor does it recognize any obedience that does not spring from faith. The two are at opposite sides of the same coin."

-A.W. Tozer

Do you ever wonder why God chose Mary to be Jesus' mommy? What did He see in her that made her so highly favored? Did she study the Scriptures even though she was female? Did she obey her parents flawlessly? She must have had faults since no one is without sin, so what made Him pick her?

<u>Luke 1:26-38</u>

[26] In the sixth month of Elizabeth's pregnancy, God sent the angel Gabriel to Nazareth, a village in Galilee, [27] to a virgin named Mary. She was engaged to be married to a man named Joseph, a descendant of King David. [28] Gabriel appeared to her and said, "Greetings, favored woman! The Lord is with you!"

[29] Confused and disturbed, Mary tried to think what the angel could mean. [30] "Don't be afraid, Mary," the angel told her, "for you have found favor with God! [31] You will conceive and give birth to a son, and you will name him Jesus. [32] He will be very great and will be called the Son of the Most High. The Lord God will give him the throne of his ancestor David. [33] And he will reign over Israel forever; his Kingdom will never end!"

[34] Mary asked the angel, "But how can this happen? I am a virgin."

[35] The angel replied, "The Holy Spirit will come upon you, and the power of the Most High will overshadow you. So the baby to be born will be holy, and he will be called the Son of God. [36] What's more, your relative Elizabeth has become pregnant in her old age! People used to say she was barren, but she has conceived a son and is now in her sixth month.[37] For the word of God will never fail."

[38] Mary responded, "I am the Lord's servant. May everything you have said about me come true." And then the angel left her.

The question is, how can you and I be prepared for what God has in store for us? Are we living as though we truly believe that the Lord will do what He says?

I bet you've experienced times where you're on a spiritual high. I know that I have often felt that nothing could separate me from Jesus, and then I come home from the retreat or I get a cold or an unexpected bill or, or, or. Mary was probably no different. The following is an excerpt from my journal from my years in Chicago as a missionary.

> "Then the angel left her." At some point, the *feelings* go away and obedience and faith have to pick up and carry on. Mary couldn't walk around in a bubble and touch her angel every time she got scared. She had to go through the nine months of her pregnancy without a visit from heaven, with no more assurance than me that God is with me—less because she didn't have the Holy Spirit yet. She "hurried" to see Elizabeth, and there is no doubt that she needed the older woman's comfort and reassurance badly. Maybe her own mom thought she was immoral.

What direction has God shown you that you must follow despite your circumstances? Mary had to keep her promise obediently, with no indication that she wasn't crazy for months at a time. She had to hold on to what she knew was true without further evidence.

What do you truly know? One of the memories that I return to frequently is my mission trip to Scotland with Youth with a Mission (YWAM) when I was 27. We spent the first week in a castle that was used for training. I was intensely lonely and homesick. I spent a lot of time outside in the fields talking to God. One night, sitting near some sheep and looking at the stars, I told the Lord, "I really need a hug and no one here knows me so I guess You're it." Believe it or not, I FELT an actual hug. It is one of those "proof of God" moments. God is not dead. He is alive! The following is a poem I wrote.

> Obey Me
>
> So I packed my bags and waved goodbye
>
> And He brought me to a place of peace and beauty
>
> Obey Me
>
> But I closed my eyes and drowned in pleasure
>
> And He shook His head and waited

Obey Me

So I pushed away the impure thoughts and cried

And He gave me nights of rest and dreams of glory

Obey Me

But I held on to my misery and ignored the pleas of those around me

And He found someone else who brought His love where it was needed

Obey Me

So I reached out my hand to a lonely heart and listened

And He healed the hurt and fear in me

Obey Me

But I laughed and played and avoided His words

And He got very quiet and didn't push

Obey Me

So I went to a quiet hill and poured out my heart

And He listened and comforted and wrapped His arms around me

Obey Me

Which will it be next time?

Freedom or pain?

POINTS TO PONDER:

Meditate on Mary and consider what might have helped her obey God's wishes. Which of the following promises inspire you to be obedient?

Exodus 20:6

But I lavish unfailing love for a thousand generations on those who love me and **obey** my commands.

Exodus 23:20-22

[20] "See, I am sending an angel before you to protect you on your journey and lead you safely to the place I have prepared for you. [21] Pay close attention to him, and **obey** his instructions. Do not rebel against him, for he is my representative, and he will not forgive your rebellion. [22] But if you are careful to **obey** him, following all my instructions, then I will be an enemy to your enemies, and I will oppose those who oppose you."

Deuteronomy 6:25

For we will be counted as righteous when we **obey** all the commands the Lord our God has given us.

Deuteronomy 30:10

The Lord your God will delight in you if you **obey** his voice and keep the commands and decrees written in this Book of Instruction, and if you turn to the Lord your God with all your heart and soul.

Joshua 1:7

Be strong and very courageous. Be careful to **obey** all the instructions Moses gave you. Do not deviate from them, turning either to the right or to the left. Then you will be successful in everything you do.

1 John 2:5

But those who **obey** God's word truly show how completely they love him. That is how we know we are living in him.

PRAYER:

Almighty Savior, I admit that it is often hard for me to obey Your Word. Create in me a desire to please You and give me a new outlook.

5
Fat Babies

"How many really capable men are children more than once during the day?"

-Napoleon Bonaparte

I do not think for one minute that singleness is a sign that you are not spiritually mature enough to be married. On the other hand, Paul does stress that being single gives you more time for the Lord.

> 1 Corinthians 7:34
>
> In the same way, a woman who is no longer married or has never been married can be devoted to the Lord and holy in body and in spirit. But a married woman has to think about her earthly responsibilities and how to please her husband.

You would think that being a single missionary would have guaranteed me to follow Him closely. But before I reached Chicago, I was acting like a spoiled brat. The following is an excerpt from my journal when I was still in California trying to raise support for the move.

> I had a real crisis of faith this weekend with only four guests at my first support party, none on Sunday, and five confirmed for Tuesday. I'm scared and hurt—not just worried about the money but hurt by those who haven't even called or written. I'm being humbled as I realize that subconsciously I thought that I <u>deserved</u> support because I've been a good friend and tried to serve God these many years. But I need to stop doing it my way and let God take over. I also need to stop sniveling and worrying that God won't provide the funds I need. I should pray more boldly and walk forward into the new territory He's giving me.

I related to the story of Joshua who had the hard task of divvying up the Promised Land to the 12 tribes after it was conquered.

> Joshua 17:14-18
>
> [14] The descendants of Joseph came to Joshua and asked, "Why have you given us only one portion of land as our homeland when the Lord has blessed us with so many people?"
>
> [15] Joshua replied, "If there are so many of you, and if the hill country of Ephraim is not large enough for you, clear out land for yourselves in the forest where the Perizzites and Rephaites live."

> [16] The descendants of Joseph responded, "It's true that the hill country is not large enough for us. But all the Canaanites in the lowlands have iron chariots, both those in Beth-shan and its surrounding settlements and those in the valley of Jezreel. They are too strong for us."
>
> [17] Then Joshua said to the tribes of Ephraim and Manasseh, the descendants of Joseph, "Since you are so large and strong, you will be given more than one portion. [18] The forests of the hill country will be yours as well. Clear as much of the land as you wish and take possession of its farthest corners. And you will drive out the Canaanites from the valleys, too, even though they are strong and have iron chariots."

How does Joshua answer the people who are complaining? What answer do you think they wanted?

Just like the descendants of Joseph, God wasn't going to simply drop the funding I needed on my lap. In the same way that He treated the tribes of Israel, His answer to me was to work harder and to trust Him. God gave the tribes a huge blessing of more land, but they had to clear the forests. They also had to overcome their fear of the enemy who appeared stronger than them. In my case, God was using those years in Chicago as spiritual sandpaper to prepare me for what was next.

Even after years of being a singles' leader, I behaved like a child when I had difficulty securing funding. In light of this, the passage below is painful to read!

<u>Hebrews 5:11-14</u>

> [11] There is much more we would like to say about this, but it is difficult to explain, especially since you are spiritually dull and don't seem to listen. [12] You have been believers so long now that you ought to be teaching others. Instead, you need someone to teach you again the basic things about God's word. You are like babies who need milk and cannot eat solid food. [13] For someone who lives on milk is still an infant and doesn't know how to do what is right. [14] Solid food is for those who are mature, who through training

have the skill to recognize the difference between right and wrong.

I highly recommend you go to YouTube and listen to the entire song "Fat Baby" by Amy Grant for a good laugh. When I was in singles' ministry, we held a talent show and some of the guys dressed in diapers and lip synced that song.

Here are a few signs to watch for so you can avoid being a spiritual baby (even if you are attending church regularly).

Slow to Learn Spiritual Concepts

This has nothing to do with I.Q. and everything to do with hunger and attitude. I bought my husband a shirt at Disney World. It has Mickey Mouse ears on it and says "Just because I have ears doesn't mean I'm listening." It's a common complaint that wives make, but I bet God would like to get our attention too.

Progress Does Not Match Spiritual Age

In other words, "You ought to be teaching others" from the above passage. This makes me cringe. I do still teach from time to time, but I should be discipling someone all the time.

Still Dependent on Others for Spiritual Growth

I'm sure you know someone who has left the church because they are "not being fed." If you are waiting for a sermon once a week to feed you, then you are seriously malnourished. Bob and I are part of a pro-life ministry (Life Movement), and occasionally we house young unwed mothers. As a part of these efforts, we provided a part-time home for a child for over three years. Even as a young toddler, this baby could feed herself. The Bible is our spiritual food, and we need to eat every day.

Can't Handle Advanced Teaching

There are times I get bored or antsy when a speaker goes beyond simple stories or joke telling and is delving deeper. This is a red flag for me that my walk with Christ needs repair.

Think We Have It Figured Out

God reminds us in these verses that we didn't do anything special to be chosen by Him.

Deuteronomy 7:7-8

[7] "The Lord did not set his heart on you and choose you because you were more numerous than other nations, for you were the smallest of all nations! [8] Rather, it was simply that the Lord loves you, and he was keeping the oath he had sworn to your ancestors. That is why the Lord rescued you with such a strong hand from your slavery and from the oppressive hand of Pharaoh, king of Egypt.

We can't forget that everything we have is because of Him. I had a friend in Chicago who was a new believer. She had a beautiful voice and often sang at weddings. Before beginning her first solo after getting saved, she heard a little whisper that said "pray," as she was about to head for the stage. She thought it was crazy because she was used to singing publicly. Again, she heard "pray," and again, she dismissed the thought. She got to the microphone, opened her mouth to sing, and "CROAK" was all she could produce. God doesn't usually give us such an obvious object lesson, but I'm pretty sure my friend will never again forget to pray and give thanks to God for her gift of music.

POINTS TO PONDER:

Read Joshua 17:14 again. Is there a situation in your life where you feel like saying "Why have you only given me. . . ?" Take a moment to consider what you can do to advance into the Promised Land. Your inheritance awaits.

Which of the five warning signs resonated most with you?

_____

_____

_____

What step can you take this week to work towards greater maturity?

_____

_____

_____

PRAYER:

Lord, I thank You for Your unconditional love even when I feel like I haven't earned it. Help me grow in my knowledge of You and to forgive myself when I falter.

6
Stagnant

"But God doesn't call us to be comfortable. He calls us to trust Him so completely that we are unafraid to put ourselves in situations where we will be in trouble if He doesn't come through."

-Francis Chan

It is so easy to get in a rut. We stop looking for a better job that actually excites us because the one we have is good enough. We get burned while online dating or from being set up by friends so we quit trying to meet new people. This attitude can translate into our spiritual lives as well. Thinking about being a spiritual baby, C.S. Lewis has something to say about those of us who still live on milk.

> If we consider the unblushing promises of reward and the staggering nature of the rewards promised in the Gospels, it would seem that Our Lord finds our desires not too strong, but too weak. We are half-hearted creatures, fooling about with drink and sex and ambition when infinite joy is offered us, like an ignorant child who wants to go on making mud pies in a slum because he cannot imagine what is meant by the offer of a holiday at the sea. *We are far too easily pleased.*[7]

Ouch. I have to admit it: a lot of the time, my flesh does not want to be spiritually mature. Couchsurfing is just fine, thank you very much.

Maybe you are past the milk stage, but there may still be periods in your life when you feel stagnant. I found the following passage very encouraging.

<u>Jeremiah 17:5-8</u>

[5] This is what the Lord says
"Cursed are those who put their trust in mere humans,
who rely on human strength
and turn their hearts away from the Lord.

[6] They are like stunted shrubs in the desert,
with no hope for the future.
They will live in the barren wilderness,
in an uninhabited salty land.

[7] "But blessed are those who trust in the Lord
and have made the Lord their hope and confidence.

[8] They are like trees planted along a riverbank,
with roots that reach deep into the water.
Such trees are not bothered by the heat
or worried by long months of drought.

> Their leaves stay green,
> and they never stop producing fruit.

Notice the last part in particular. Don't fret about the "long months of drought." If you "trust in the Lord and have made the Lord [your] hope and confidence," then He promises you will "never stop producing fruit." Don't you love that?

On the other hand, maybe we need a little kick to escape the doldrums. James 4:2 says "you don't have what you want because you don't ask God for it." Speaking from experience, I think it is easy for single women to not push forward in their faith. Obviously, there are many examples of just the opposite, those who like Paul are able to see their unmarried status as the perfect opportunity to do more for God. But I think that some of us tend to be complacent, not only waiting for a man but for life itself to start. I challenge you to take action. Here are a few ideas for how to make this happen.

<u>Explore Scripture</u>

Identify a topic in the Bible that you don't understand and spend a few weeks exploring it. Look up every reference, use commentaries, and pray for guidance. But remember, reading the word doesn't change you any more than looking at a mirror will brush your hair. It only shows you where you can change.

<u>Get Outside!</u>

Nature is a powerful tool. Eden was a garden after all.

> <u>Psalm 19:1-4 (Psalms Now)</u>
>
> Wherever I am, wherever I go,
> I can sense something of the power of God.
> The grandeur of the mountains,
> the vastness of the oceans,
> the breathtaking wonder of interstellar space;
> all this proclaims thee glory and majesty of God.
> Even amid the clutter of our cities,
> built and abused by the hands of men,
> there are reflections of divine splendor.
> Heaven's silence or earth's clamor
> may not be very articulate.

Yet God's voice can be heard.
He makes His presence known throughout the world.

Go for a walk or, if possible, get away for a weekend to a lake, mountain, or a beach, etc. If that is not feasible, just go outside at night and look at the stars.

Read a Christian Book

Try anything by Philip Yancy or Max Lucado or Kay Arthur or Beth Moore or a Christian classic like *The Screwtape Letters* by C.S. Lewis. Underline and journal as you read. Also, try a different translation for your Bible devotions. Sometimes a paraphrase like *The Message* can awaken your heart.

Make a Date with Jesus

I do NOT mean quiet time. When I first moved to Chicago, I was desperately lonely. I love to sightsee, so every Saturday, I would pick a new location to explore like the zoo or Lakeshore Beach, and I would take a long walk. I asked Jesus to come along as my companion since I had no one else. It was very low key, but trying to be aware of His presence with me was incredibly helpful.

Teach Someone

The difference between a river and a swamp is that a river has an outlet. Don't keep what you learn to yourself. I volunteered many times for my church's Sunday School program. I was out of my comfort zone, nut through this experience, I learned which age groups are difficult for me (young teens and 3-5-year-olds) and those with which I am actually able to engage (middle school).

Invest Time in Friendship with a Nonbeliever

After years of asking my actress friend to join a Bible study, she finally said yes. Afterward, she was ready for more, and we spent years studying together and talking about everything.

Commit to Being a Good Friend

Whatever you do, don't let yourself become isolated. In the story of the demon-possessed man (Luke 8:26-39), the enemy of our souls drives him "into solitary places" (NIV) to "live among the tombs"

(NLT). This is an extreme example of isolation, but the point is to stay in relationships and give your heart to some girlfriends. It's worth the risk.

Go on a Mission Trip

If your church does not sponsor mission trips, ask around at other local churches or check out Youth with a Mission. I was fortunate that my San Diego church singles' group went to an orphanage in Tijuana, Mexico once a month. Later I spent a month in Scotland with YWAM. There is nothing like a mission trip to pump you up spiritually and grow your faith past the milk stage.

Speaking of missions, before going to Chicago, I called the mission board of a well-known denomination. I wanted to see what their policy was for applying to the mission field. On the phone, without knowing me whatsoever, I was denied even the right to apply because I was "too old" (40) to learn the skills I needed to go on the trip, specifically another language. I had just graduated with my Master's Degree in Theology where I had studied Greek. I bet the interviewer didn't speak Greek!

POINTS TO PONDER:

Do you find yourself being "far too easily pleased" in your relationship with Jesus? What do you think is holding you back from pursuing His love more deeply?

Highlight one of the eight action points above and schedule a time to try it.

PRAYER:

Yahweh, my heart wants to follow You wherever You want to take me, but my flesh is scared of what You may ask. Help me understand that You are a gentleman who will lead me at a pace I can handle.

7
Fear

"The wise man in the storm prays to God, not for safety from danger, but for deliverance from fear. It is the storm within which endangers him, not the storm without."

-Ralph Waldo Emerson

I heard a sermon by Gary Jones at my San Diego church, and he said that fear is **F**alse **E**xpectations **A**ppearing **R**eal. I think that fear of the future was the greatest obstacle I faced in my life as a single woman. Because, truthfully, day-to-day living was fairly enjoyable. I had friends, I had hobbies and interests, and to be brutally honest, I had more freedom then than I do now. But I worried constantly about the days to come. How would I survive being alone at 40? 60? 80? I wish I had known this verse then: "He will not fear bad news; his heart is steadfast, trusting [confidently relying on and believing] in the Lord" (Psalm 112:7, Amplified Bible).

Let's explore the topic of fear and try to understand how we can trust God. To begin, Proverbs 29:25 provides some excellent wisdom. "Fearing people is a dangerous trap, but trusting the Lord means safety." After all, "The Lord is for me, so I will have no fear. What can mere people do to me?" (Psalm 118:6).

This is hardly an original idea, but it works well. Try personalizing Scriptures. This is my version of Isaiah 44:2: "The Lord who made me and helps me says: 'Do not be afraid, Janan, my servant, O dear daughter, my chosen one.'"

Results of Fear

<u>Stops You in Your Tracks</u>

2 Samuel 17:10 says, "Then even the bravest soldiers, though they have the heart of a lion, will be paralyzed with fear." If the devil can keep you from doing what God has called you to do out of fear, he has gained a victory.

There are 219 passages in the New Living Translation Bible that contain the word "afraid" and 330 verses about "fear." It is obviously a universal problem. Let's absorb what God is telling us through the prophet Isaiah.

<u>Isaiah 41:9b-13</u>

[9b] For I have chosen you
and will not throw you away.
[10] Don't be afraid, for I am with you.

Don't be discouraged, for I am your God.
I will strengthen you and help you.
I will hold you up with my victorious right hand.
[11] "See, all your angry enemies lie there,
confused and humiliated.
Anyone who opposes you will die
and come to nothing.
[12] You will look in vain
for those who tried to conquer you.
Those who attack you
will come to nothing.
[13] For I hold you by your right hand—
I, the Lord your God.
And I say to you,
'Don't be afraid. I am here to help you.'

Prevents You from Being Used by God

1 Chronicles 28:20

> Then David continued, "Be strong and courageous, and do the work. Don't be afraid or discouraged, for the Lord God, my God, is with you. He will not fail you or forsake you. He will see to it that all the work related to the Temple of the Lord is finished correctly."

I really love this promise. "He will see to it that all the work... is finished correctly.'" Do you have tasks to complete for the Lord, but you are inhibited by fear? If you are following in His footsteps and doing what He has asked you to do, then hang on to this verse. I was terrified when I arrived in Chicago. The following advice helped me.

> Some people say, "God will never ask me to do something I can't do." I have come to the place in my life that, if the assignment I sense God is giving me is something that I know I can handle, I know it probably is *not* from God. The assignments God gives in the Bible are always God-sized. They are always beyond what people can do because He wants to demonstrate His nature, His strength, His provision, and His kindness to His people and to a watching world.[8]

Keeps Your Mouth Shut

John 12:42-43

² Many people did believe in him, however, including some of the Jewish leaders. But they wouldn't admit it for fear that the Pharisees would expel them from the synagogue. ⁴³ For they loved human praise more than the praise of God.

Uh oh. I don't want fewer people to go to heaven because of my fear, but unfortunately, most of us suffer from anxiety about being open about our faith. Consider this thought though. If you conquer your fear, your faith will be contagious.

Philippians 1:13-14

¹³ For everyone here, including the whole palace guard, knows that I am in chains because of Christ. 14 And because of my imprisonment, most of the believers here have gained confidence and boldly speak God's message without fear.

How can you personalize the above passage? Because of my_____ then _____. My husband has been partially paralyzed since 1987. I have seen time and time again where *because* of his being in a wheelchair and yet radiating joy, people stop and ask questions. In these exchanges, they get a little glimpse of the power of Jesus.

Hampers Communication with God

On Mount Sinai, fear kept the people from approaching God.

Exodus 20:18-19

¹⁸ When the people heard the thunder and the loud blast of the ram's horn, and when they saw the flashes of lightning and the smoke billowing from the mountain, they stood at a distance, trembling with fear.

¹⁹ And they said to Moses, "You speak to us, and we will listen. But don't let God speak directly to us, or we will die!"

Examine your heart to see if you are maybe secretly afraid of what God might say to You if you let Him in all the way.

Compromises Integrity

Genesis 12:10-19

¹⁰ At that time a severe famine struck the land of Canaan, forcing Abram to go down to Egypt, where he lived as a foreigner. ¹¹ As he was approaching the border of Egypt, Abram said to his wife, Sarai, "Look, you are a very beautiful woman. ¹² When the Egyptians see you, they will say, 'This is his wife. Let's kill him; then we can have her!' ¹³ So please tell them you are my sister. Then they will spare my life and treat me well because of their interest in you."

¹⁴ And sure enough, when Abram arrived in Egypt, everyone noticed Sarai's beauty. ¹⁵ When the palace officials saw her, they sang her praises to Pharaoh, their king, and Sarai was taken into his palace. ¹⁶ Then Pharaoh gave Abram many gifts because of her—sheep, goats, cattle, male and female donkeys, male and female servants, and camels.

¹⁷ But the Lord sent terrible plagues upon Pharaoh and his household because of Sarai, Abram's wife. ¹⁸ So Pharaoh summoned Abram and accused him sharply. "What have you done to me?" he demanded. "Why didn't you tell me she was your wife? ¹⁹ Why did you say, 'She is my sister,' and allow me to take her as my wife? Now then, here is your wife. Take her and get out of here!"

Pharaoh was naturally furious with Abram when he discovered his deception. Abram had acted out of fear and not faith.

Promotes Insecurity[9]

John 20:20-25 describes how the disciples are hiding behind locked doors *after* the Resurrection. The concept of Jesus returning from the dead was mind blowing and they hid. What might you be missing because of your fear of the unknown?

Causes Stagnation[10]

This is the most heartbreaking result of fear. Even after the spies went into the Promised Land and came back with a wonderful report, people were afraid.

Deuteronomy 1:26-33 (The Message)

²⁶⁻²⁸ But then you weren't willing to go up. You rebelled against God, your God's plain word. You complained in your tents: "God hates us. He hauled us out of Egypt in order to dump us among the Amorites—a death sentence for sure! How can we go up? We're trapped in a dead end. Our brothers took all the wind out of our sails, telling us, 'The people are bigger and stronger than we are; their cities are huge, their defenses massive—we even saw Anakite giants there!'"

²⁹⁻³³ I tried to relieve your fears: "Don't be terrified of them. God, your God, is leading the way; he's fighting for you. You saw with your own eyes what he did for you in Egypt; you saw what he did in the wilderness, how God, your God, carried you as a father carries his child, carried you the whole way until you arrived here. But now that you're here, you won't trust God, your God—this same God who goes ahead of you in your travels to scout out a place to pitch camp, a fire by night and a cloud by day to show you the way to go."

³⁴⁻³⁶ When God heard what you said, he exploded in anger. He swore, "Not a single person of this evil generation is going to get so much as a look at the good land that I promised to give to your parents. Not one—except for Caleb son of Jephunneh. He'll see it. I'll give him and his descendants the land he walked on because he was all for following God, heart and soul."

It's easy for us to read these stories and think "Come on, guys! Remember the parting of the Red Sea? Where's your faith?" Think back on a time when your own prayers have been answered and write down a few times when God came through to boost your morale. Remember this the next time you begin to doubt Him.

Reasons Not to Fear

The entire Bible gives us reasons to not fear.

Many Promises

Proverbs 1:33

But all who listen to me will live in peace, untroubled by fear of harm.

Proverbs 3:24

You can go to bed without fear; you will lie down and sleep soundly.

Romans 8:38

And I am convinced that nothing can ever separate us from God's love. Neither death nor life, neither angels nor demons, neither our fears for today nor our worries about tomorrow—not even the powers of hell can separate us from God's love.

Don't Miss an Opportunity

Exodus 2:5-9

[5] Soon Pharaoh's daughter came down to bathe in the river, and her attendants walked along the riverbank. When the princess saw the basket among the reeds, she sent her maid to get it for her. [6] When the princess opened it, she saw the baby. The little boy was crying, and she felt sorry for him. "This must be one of the Hebrew children," she said.

[7] Then the baby's sister approached the princess. "Should I go and find one of the Hebrew women to nurse the baby for you?" she asked.

[8] "Yes, do!" the princess replied. So the girl went and called the baby's mother.

[9] "Take this baby and nurse him for me," the princess told the baby's mother. "I will pay you for your help." So the woman took her baby home and nursed him.

If Moses' sister Miriam had allowed fear of being caught to take over, the entire Old Testament would be different. Keep your eyes open to what God may be asking you to do that is outside your comfort zone.

You Are Not Alone

2 Kings 6:15-17

[15] When the servant of the man of God got up early the next morning and went outside, there were troops, horses, and

chariots everywhere. "Oh, sir, what will we do now?" the young man cried to Elisha.

¹⁶ "Don't be afraid!" Elisha told him. "For there are more on our side than on theirs!" ¹⁷ Then Elisha prayed, "O Lord, open his eyes and let him see!" The Lord opened the young man's eyes, and when he looked up, he saw that the hillside around Elisha was filled with horses and chariots of fire.

Not only are there angels on your side, but I bet you have more resources than you are utilizing. Set your pride down and call a friend or a pastor or join a book club or small group.

POINTS TO PONDER:

Meditate on the following verse. From what fear do you want deliverance?

> 1 John 4:18 (Amplified Bible)
>
> There is no fear in love [dread does not exist]. But perfect (complete, full-grown) love drives out fear, because fear involves [the expectation of divine] punishment, so the one who is afraid [of God's judgment] is not perfected in love [has not grown into a sufficient understanding of God's love].

PRAYER:

Sovereign God, I want to trust You absolutely and be unafraid. Reveal the source of my fears to me and help me to overcome them.

8
FEAR PART 2

"I'm not afraid of storms for
I'm learning how to sail my ship."

-LOUISA MAY ALCOTT

How to Handle Fear

<u>Pray!</u>

Well, duh. Of course, prayer should be the first response to fear. Remember the story of how Jacob cheated his brother Esau out of his birthright? Now, Jacob is about to come face-to-face with him after many years apart. He is anxious. Read on to see how he handled it.

<u>Genesis 32:3-12</u>

³ Then Jacob sent messengers ahead to his brother, Esau, who was living in the region of Seir in the land of Edom. ⁴ He told them, "Give this message to my master Esau: 'Humble greetings from your servant Jacob. Until now I have been living with Uncle Laban, ⁵ and now I own cattle, donkeys, flocks of sheep and goats, and many servants, both men and women. I have sent these messengers to inform my lord of my coming, hoping that you will be friendly to me.'"

⁶ After delivering the message, the messengers returned to Jacob and reported, "We met your brother, Esau, and he is already on his way to meet you—with an army of 400 men!" ⁷ Jacob was terrified at the news. He divided his household, along with the flocks and herds and camels, into two groups. ⁸ He thought, "If Esau meets one group and attacks it, perhaps the other group can escape."

⁹ Then Jacob prayed, "O God of my grandfather Abraham, and God of my father, Isaac—O Lord, you told me, 'Return to your own land and to your relatives.' And you promised me, 'I will treat you kindly.' ¹⁰ I am not worthy of all the unfailing love and faithfulness you have shown to me, your servant. When I left home and crossed the Jordan River, I owned nothing except a walking stick. Now my household fills two large camps! ¹¹ O Lord, please rescue me from the hand of my brother, Esau. I am afraid that he is coming to attack me, along with my wives and children. ¹² But you promised me, 'I will surely treat you kindly, and I will multiply your descendants until they become as numerous as the sands along the seashore—too many to count.'"

Accept Change

It is perfectly natural to dread the unknown. I find it comforting that God doesn't rebuke us but promises His presence instead.

Genesis 46:1-4

¹ So Jacob set out for Egypt with all his possessions. And when he came to Beersheba, he offered sacrifices to the God of his father, Isaac. ² During the night God spoke to him in a vision. "Jacob! Jacob!" he called.

"Here I am," Jacob replied.

³ "I am God, the God of your father," the voice said. "Do not be afraid to go down to Egypt, for there I will make your family into a great nation. ⁴ I will go with you down to Egypt, and I will bring you back again. You will die in Egypt, but Joseph will be with you to close your eyes."

Remember God's Names

Psalm 24:8

Who is the King of glory?
The Lord, strong and mighty;
the Lord, invincible in battle.

God's name in the above verse (Jehovah Gibbor Milchamah) means The Lord Mighty in Battle. The translation of His name below (Jehovah Chereb) means The Lord the Sword.

Deuteronomy 23:29

How blessed you are, O Israel!
Who else is like you, a people saved by the Lord?
He is your protecting shield
and your triumphant sword!
Your enemies will cringe before you,
and you will stomp on their backs!

I have recently been studying a few of the over 900 names of God in Scripture. I believe that knowing which name to call on for your particular situation enhances your prayer. Doesn't it make you feel braver knowing that the One who is mighty in battle and carries a triumphant sword is on your side?

<u>Exodus 14:10-14</u>

[10] As Pharaoh approached, the people of Israel looked up and panicked when they saw the Egyptians overtaking them. They cried out to the Lord, [11] and they said to Moses, "Why did you bring us out here to die in the wilderness? Weren't there enough graves for us in Egypt? What have you done to us? Why did you make us leave Egypt? [12] Didn't we tell you this would happen while we were still in Egypt? We said, 'Leave us alone! Let us be slaves to the Egyptians. It's better to be a slave in Egypt than a corpse in the wilderness!'"

[13] But Moses told the people, "Don't be afraid. Just stand still and watch the Lord rescue you today. The Egyptians you see today will never be seen again. [14] The Lord himself will fight for you. Just stay calm."

I am not a Downton Abbey fan, but the last verse caught my eye. It is good advice.

<u>Be Loud and Proud</u>

<u>1 Samuel 14:6-20</u>

[6] "Let's go across to the outpost of those pagans," Jonathan said to his armor bearer. "Perhaps the Lord will help us, for nothing can hinder the Lord. He can win a battle whether he has many warriors or only a few!"

I like how Jonathan proclaims his faith out loud. Our very good friends Steve and Jan taught Bob and me a great deal about *not* verbalizing the negative but making a point of speaking only in faith. Grab your Bible and finish the story to see how his faith played out.

<u>Stay in the Word</u>

Being told to read the Bible daily gets old, I know. When it feels like a religious obligation and there is no joy involved, there seems to be little point in doing it. But without knowing His Word you are abandoning your greatest tool, not just for fighting fear but for being successful in all you do.

Joshua 1:6-9

⁶ Be strong and courageous, for you are the one who will lead these people to possess all the land I swore to their ancestors I would give them. ⁷ Be strong and very courageous. Be careful to obey all the instructions Moses gave you. Do not deviate from them, turning either to the right or to the left. Then you will be successful in everything you do. ⁸ Study this Book of Instruction continually. Meditate on it day and night so you will be sure to obey everything written in it. Only then will you prosper and succeed in all you do. ⁹ This is my command—be strong and courageous! Do not be afraid or discouraged. For the Lord your God is with you wherever you go."

Face It Head On

Out of 30 trusted and mighty warriors, David had three friends in whom he confided the most. One friend especially came through for him.

1 Chronicles 11:12-14

¹² Next in rank among the Three was Eleazar son of Dodai, a descendant of Ahoah. ¹³ He was with David when the Philistines gathered for battle at Pas-dammim and attacked the Israelites in a field full of barley. The Israelite army fled, ¹⁴ but Eleazar and David held their ground in the middle of the field and beat back the Philistines. So the Lord saved them by giving them a great victory.

It takes discernment to know whether this is a fight in which God is calling you to hold your ground and watch Him bring victory.

React Instantly

Nehemiah 2:1-6

¹ Early the following spring, in the month of Nisan, during the twentieth year of King Artaxerxes' reign, I was serving the king his wine. I had never before appeared sad in his

presence. ² So the king asked me, "Why are you looking so sad? You don't look sick to me. You must be deeply troubled."

Then I was terrified, ³ but I replied, "Long live the king! How can I not be sad? For the city where my ancestors are buried is in ruins, and the gates have been destroyed by fire."

⁴ The king asked, "Well, how can I help you?"

With a prayer to the God of heaven, ⁵ I replied, "If it please the king, and if you are pleased with me, your servant, send me to Judah to rebuild the city where my ancestors are buried."

⁶ The king, with the queen sitting beside him, asked, "How long will you be gone? When will you return?" After I told him how long I would be gone, the king agreed to my request.

Nehemiah was "terrified" to speak honestly to his employer but responded "with a prayer," successfully petitioning the king.

POINTS TO PONDER:

Remember how Eleazar stood with David in battle. Have you sought a friend to keep you company in prayer when you are afraid or doubtful? Keeping your fear to yourself will only strengthen the enemy's hold on your mind.

PRAYER:

O Lord, I praise You for being the Sword and Mighty in Battle. I will turn to You for protection the next time fear strikes me and wait for Your victory.

9
FOCUS ON THE TRUE GOD

"If you believe in a God who controls the big things, you have to believe in a God who controls the little things. It is we, of course, to whom things look 'little' or 'big'."

-ELISABETH ELLIOT

The reason for this chapter is self-explanatory. It may be the fact that you are single or it may be your finances or your desire for a more fulfilling career. It could be a less-than-perfect relationship with your parents. Often, we get so focused on what is "wrong" with our lives that we forget the blessings and the abundance of our HUGE God.

The story below is one of the most amazing miracles in the Bible. I had the great good fortune to travel to Israel with my church group (taking side trips to Amsterdam, Cairo, and Rome) when I was in my 30s. One of my favorite places was Mt. Carmel. Perhaps because landscapes aren't as varied as cities, I truly felt the Lord's presence on that mountain, imagining Elijah standing on the same peak and challenging the enemy with such boldness.

<u>1 Kings 18:20-39</u>

[20] So Ahab summoned all the people of Israel and the prophets to Mount Carmel. [21] Then Elijah stood in front of them and said, "How much longer will you waver, hobbling between two opinions? If the Lord is God, follow him! But if Baal is God, then follow him!" But the people were completely silent.

[22] Then Elijah said to them, "I am the only prophet of the Lord who is left, but Baal has 450 prophets. [23] Now bring two bulls. The prophets of Baal may choose whichever one they wish and cut it into pieces and lay it on the wood of their altar, but without setting fire to it. I will prepare the other bull and lay it on the wood on the altar, but not set fire to it.[24] Then call on the name of your god, and I will call on the name of the Lord. The god who answers by setting fire to the wood is the true God!" And all the people agreed.

[25] Then Elijah said to the prophets of Baal, "You go first, for there are many of you. Choose one of the bulls, and prepare it and call on the name of your god. But do not set fire to the wood."

[26] So they prepared one of the bulls and placed it on the altar. Then they called on the name of Baal from morning until noontime, shouting, "O Baal, answer us!" But there was no

reply of any kind. Then they danced, hobbling around the altar they had made.

[27] About noontime Elijah began mocking them. "You'll have to shout louder," he scoffed, "for surely he is a god! Perhaps he is daydreaming, or is relieving himself. Or maybe he is away on a trip, or is asleep and needs to be wakened!"

[28] So they shouted louder, and following their normal custom, they cut themselves with knives and swords until the blood gushed out. [29] They raved all afternoon until the time of the evening sacrifice, but still there was no sound, no reply, no response.

[30] Then Elijah called to the people, "Come over here!" They all crowded around him as he repaired the altar of the Lord that had been torn down. [31] He took twelve stones, one to represent each of the tribes of Israel, [32] and he used the stones to rebuild the altar in the name of the Lord. Then he dug a trench around the altar large enough to hold about three gallons. [33] He piled wood on the altar, cut the bull into pieces, and laid the pieces on the wood.

Then he said, "Fill four large jars with water, and pour the water over the offering and the wood."

[34] After they had done this, he said, "Do the same thing again!" And when they were finished, he said, "Now do it a third time!" So they did as he said, [35] and the water ran around the altar and even filled the trench.

[36] At the usual time for offering the evening sacrifice, Elijah the prophet walked up to the altar and prayed, "O Lord, God of Abraham, Isaac, and Jacob, prove today that you are God in Israel and that I am your servant. Prove that I have done all this at your command. [37] O Lord, answer me! Answer me so these people will know that you, O Lord, are God and that you have brought them back to yourself."

[38] Immediately the fire of the Lord flashed down from heaven and burned up the young bull, the wood, the stones, and the dust. It even licked up all the water in the trench! [39]

And when all the people saw it, they fell face down on the ground and cried out, "The Lord —he is God! Yes, the Lord is God!"

For me and perhaps other Christians today, I am so happy to have Jesus as my best friend that I become too comfortable with Him. I do not attend a liturgical church, but when I do visit, I admit that there is something powerful in the reverence that is shown. Once, I was invited to a coworker's wedding. It was tedious and boring, and I was beginning to squirm. At one point, the priest did a long prayer. Every time he paused, the congregation repeated, "Lord, have mercy on me." The first ten times or so I said the phrase, it was just meaningless repetition, as the Bible warns us. But after it went on and on, the phrase caught hold of my spirit and pretty soon I was in tears. By then I meant every word: *"Lord, have mercy on me."*

Somehow, I need to balance my coziness with my buddy Jesus with the knowledge of The Lord He Is GOD! Read the following Psalms out loud, and keep them on hand for the days when you need to acknowledge His power.

Psalm 99:1-3

¹ The Lord is king!
Let the nations tremble!
He sits on his throne between the cherubim.
Let the whole earth quake!
² The Lord sits in majesty in Jerusalem,
exalted above all the nations.
³ Let them praise your great and awesome name.
Your name is holy!

Psalm 97:1-6
¹ The Lord is king!
Let the earth rejoice!
Let the farthest coastlands be glad.
² Dark clouds surround him.
Righteousness and justice are the foundation of his throne.
³ Fire spreads ahead of him

and burns up all his foes.
⁴His lightning flashes out across the world.
The earth sees and trembles.
⁵The mountains melt like wax before the Lord,
before the Lord of all the earth.
⁶The heavens proclaim his righteousness;
every nation sees his glory.

POINTS TO PONDER:

What causes you to lose focus on the true God? The Israelites did not completely reject God. They believed in Him, but their faith was diluted by interacting with the worshippers of Baal around them—much like our involvement with the modern world and its many distractions.

PRAYER:

El Shaddai, Mighty God, You are so awesome and immense and powerful that I want to fall to my knees and hide my face. I am humbled to realize that You seek a relationship with me. Help me to balance my awe of You with my comfort in approaching Your throne.

10
Out of Focus

"You will never reach your destination
if you stop and throw stones at every
dog that barks."

-Winston Churchill

No matter how strong our faith in Christ is, it is difficult to consistently stay focused on Him. To identify roadblocks, read the following verses, and use the chart below to list some things that are *not* helpful when trying to focus. This exercise will also help you to identify tools for staying on track.

Romans 4:19-25 (The Message)

Abraham didn't focus on his own impotence and say, "It's hopeless. This hundred-year-old body could never father a child." Nor did he survey Sarah's decades of infertility and give up. He didn't tiptoe around God's promise asking cautiously skeptical questions. He plunged into the promise and came up strong, ready for God, sure that God would make good on what he had said. That's why it is said, "Abraham was declared fit before God by trusting God to set him right." But it's not just Abraham; it's also us! The same thing gets said about us when we embrace and believe the One who brought Jesus to life when the conditions were equally hopeless. The sacrificed Jesus made us fit for God, set us *right with God*.

Romans 8:5-8 (The Message)

Those who think they can do it on their own end up obsessed with measuring their own moral muscle but never get around to exercising it in real life. Those who trust God's action in them find that God's Spirit is in them—living and breathing God! Obsession with self in these matters is a dead end; attention to God leads us out into the open, into a spacious, free life. Focusing on the self is the opposite of focusing on God. Anyone completely absorbed in self ignores God, ends up thinking more about self than God. That person ignores who God is and what he is doing. And God isn't pleased at being ignored.

2 Corinthians 5:14-15 (The Message)

Our firm decision is to work from this focused center: One man died for everyone. That puts everyone in the same boat. He included everyone in his death so that everyone could also be included in his life, a resurrection life, a far better life than people ever lived on their own.

Galatians 3:1 (The Message)

You crazy Galatians! Did someone put a hex on you? Have you taken leave of your senses? Something crazy has happened, for it's obvious that you no longer have the crucified Jesus in clear focus in your lives. His sacrifice on the cross was certainly set before you clearly enough.

2 Peter 1:16-19 (The Message)

We weren't, you know, just wishing on a star when we laid the facts out before you regarding the powerful return of our Master, Jesus Christ. We were there for the preview! We saw it with our own eyes: Jesus resplendent with light from God the Father as the voice of Majestic Glory spoke: "This is my Son, marked by my love, focus of all my delight." We were there on the holy mountain with him. We heard the voice out of heaven with our very own ears.

[19-21] We couldn't be more sure of what we saw and heard—*God's* glory, *God's* voice. The prophetic Word was confirmed to us. You'll do well to keep focusing on it. It's the one light you have in a dark time as you wait for daybreak and the rising of the Morning Star in your hearts.

Psalm 119:65-72 (The Message)

Be good to your servant, God; be as good as your Word. Train me in good common sense; I'm thoroughly committed to living your way. Before I learned to answer you, I wandered all over the place, but now I'm in step with your Word. You are good, and the source of good; train me in your goodness. The godless spread lies about me, but I focus my attention on what you are saying; They're bland as a bucket of lard, while I dance to the tune of your revelation. My troubles turned out all for the best—they forced me to learn from your textbook. Truth from your mouth means more to me than striking it rich in a gold mine.

1 Timothy 4:12-14

[12] Don't let anyone think less of you because you are young. Be an example to all believers in what you say, in the way you live, in your love, your faith, and your purity. [13] Until

I get there, focus on reading the Scriptures to the church, encouraging the believers, and teaching them.

[14] Do not neglect the spiritual gift you received through the prophecy spoken over you when the elders of the church laid their hands on you.

Matthew 6:6 (The Message)

Here's what I want you to do: Find a quiet, secluded place so you won't be tempted to role-play before God. Just be there as simply and honestly as you can manage. The focus will shift from you to God, and you will begin to sense his grace.

	DON'T FOCUS	FOCUS ON
Romans 4		
Romans 8		
2 Corinthians		
Galatians		
2 Peter		Word
Psalm		
1 Timothy	Your inability	
Matthew		

I hope the verses above help you focus on Christ. It is a daily goal, one that I don't think will ever become automatic for me. This is my journal entry from when the concept first became clear to me.

> My new direction is to focus on Jesus Christ—instead of trying to fix myself, trying to make myself holy and feeling constantly guilty because I am so far from that ideal. I'm going to walk closer to Jesus so that I can see His face.

POINTS TO PONDER:

Identify your favorite Scripture above and sit for a few moments and just dwell in it. For example, I would choose the passage from Romans 4, and my meditation would be something like this:

Lord, help me to not focus on my failings. If Abram had only looked at his age and inability to have a child, You would not have been free to accomplish a miracle. I know my faults too well, that I am lazy and sometimes too shy and not terribly bold or motivated to do Your work. Help me "plunge into the promise" like my spiritual forefather and focus on Your power and strength instead of my own lack.

PRAYER:

Light of the World, light up my life with Your promises. This week, remind me about the things that distract me from You. Give me the courage to put my foot down and say "NO!" to temptations and "YES!" to Your presence.

11
Prayer Misconceptions

"Next to the wonder of seeing my Savior will be, I think, the wonder that I made so little use of the power of prayer."

-Dwight L. Moody

Below, I include some wrong ideas about prayer that even seasoned Christians may still harbor. You may recognize your own doubts or find something useful to share with a struggling friend.

"If It Be Thy Will"

How often have you heard this uttered in a group prayer session? It sounds so spiritual and submissive, but the problem is that it isn't biblical. Richard J. Foster tells us that Jesus and the disciples *never* prayed "if it be Thy will."

> They obviously believed that they knew what the will of God was before they prayed the prayer of faith. They were so immersed in the milieu of the Holy Spirit that when they encountered a specific situation, they knew it should be done. Their praying was so positive that it often took the form of a direct, authoritative command: "Walk," "Be well," "Stand up." I saw that when praying for others there was evidently no room for indecisive, tentative, half-hoping, "if it be Thy will" prayers.[11]

The only similar instance of this phrase in the Bible is when Jesus moans in the garden of Gethsemane.

Luke 22:39-42 (NIV)

> [39] Jesus went out as usual to the Mount of Olives, and his disciples followed him. [40] On reaching the place, he said to them, "Pray that you will not fall into temptation." [41] He withdrew about a stone's throw beyond them, knelt down and prayed, [42] "Father, if you are willing, take this cup from me; yet not my will, but yours be done."

This is obviously a very different circumstance than when we are praying for someone else or for our own needs. We should imitate Jesus who knew the Father's heart and was confident of the things He wanted to accomplish. He said "Walk!" and "Stand!" and "Be healed!" without any disclaimers.

If what you are asking is in line with the Lord's desire, which includes abundant life, health, peace, and joy, then pray boldly.

"I'm Too Angry to Pray"

First of all, do you really think that God doesn't already know how you feel? There is no need to present Him with the superhero version of you. The real you is who He redeemed on the cross.

Secondly, how would you feel if your best friend refused to talk to you? Wouldn't you rather have open communication than being given the silent treatment?

Job 7:11

Therefore I will not keep silent;
I will speak out in the anguish of my spirit,
I will complain in the bitterness of my soul.

It is amazing to me that when the heroes of the Bible are very blunt with God, they end up having an attitude adjustment. In the following Psalms, David begins in great anger. However, I believe that coming into the presence of God honestly changed him, and it will also refine us.

Psalm 13:1-6

¹ O Lord, how long will you forget me? Forever?
How long will you look the other way?
² How long must I struggle with anguish in my soul,
with sorrow in my heart every day?
How long will my enemy have the upper hand?

³ Turn and answer me, O Lord my God!
Restore the sparkle to my eyes, or I will die.
⁴ Don't let my enemies gloat, saying, "We have defeated him!"
Don't let them rejoice at my downfall.
⁵ But I trust in your unfailing love.
I will rejoice because you have rescued me.
⁶ I will sing to the Lord
because he is good to me.

Psalm 73:12-26

¹² Look at these wicked people—
enjoying a life of ease while their riches multiply.

¹³ Did I keep my heart pure for nothing?
Did I keep myself innocent for no reason?
¹⁴ I get nothing but trouble all day long;
every morning brings me pain.

¹⁵ If I had really spoken this way to others,
I would have been a traitor to your people.
¹⁶ So I tried to understand why the wicked prosper.
But what a difficult task it is!
¹⁷ Then I went into your sanctuary, O God,
and I finally understood the destiny of the wicked.
¹⁸ Truly, you put them on a slippery path
and send them sliding over the cliff to destruction.
¹⁹ In an instant they are destroyed,
completely swept away by terrors.
²⁰ When you arise, O Lord,
you will laugh at their silly ideas
as a person laughs at dreams in the morning.

²¹ Then I realized that my heart was bitter,
and I was all torn up inside.
²² I was so foolish and ignorant—
I must have seemed like a senseless animal to you.
²³ Yet I still belong to you;
you hold my right hand.
²⁴ You guide me with your counsel,
leading me to a glorious destiny.
²⁵ Whom have I in heaven but you?
I desire you more than anything on earth.
²⁶ My health may fail, and my spirit may grow weak,
but God remains the strength of my heart;
he is mine forever.

Lastly, think about how Jesus handled great emotions. Continuing in Luke from the above passage, it says that Jesus, *"being in anguish, he prayed more earnestly,* and his sweat was like drops of blood falling to the ground" (Luke 22:44). Let the storm of your feelings drive you towards God, not away from Him.

"God is Too Busy"

I remember having countless discussions with friends in San Diego about parking spaces. My girlfriend always prayed for a space to open up if we were running late or it was raining, etc. Another friend thought that she was using the Lord like a genie in a bottle and that it was bordering on being disrespectful.

How do you think Jesus feels about the "little" things in your life? We know that He cared enough to feed a crowd of 5,000 hungry people, so a meal was not too small of a concern. I was a very baby Christian when I dropped my contact lens in the grass, and it was impossible for me to find it. My friend who was a little further along in her faith told me to pray about it, and I thought she was nuts. But I took her advice, and sure enough, my contact appeared.

My favorite example of this is when my friend Lisa's dad died, and I flew to Ohio for his funeral. Lisa was my best friend in high school. She moved east, and I went to college in Stockton, CA. I got a call in the middle of the night that her dad had died suddenly. I had finals, I was rehearsing in a play, but I woke my dad up, and he agreed to wire me some money for a morning flight. (Remember that this was before every teen had a cell phone and a credit card.) I woke up a friend to ask for a ride to the airport. In the hallway of our co-ed dorm, a guy I barely knew asked me why I was crying. He stepped away for a moment before returning with a check for $500 made out to me. He said to pay him back whenever I could. I told him I didn't need it, but he insisted. It turned out that the office that had my wired money didn't open until after my flight had left. God *is* in the details of your day-to-day existence.

"If You Do This Then I Will. . ."

We have all been tempted to try to enroll in the Divine Insurance Policy several weeks before a major life event or decision. We barter and beg, but be careful!

Ecclesiastes 5:1-5

> As you enter the house of God, keep your ears open and your mouth shut. It is evil to make mindless offerings to God. ² Don't make rash promises, and don't be hasty in bringing matters before God. After all, God is in heaven,

and you are here on earth. So let your words be few. ³ Too much activity gives you restless dreams; too many words make you a fool. ⁴ When you make a promise to God, don't delay in following through, for God takes no pleasure in fools. Keep all the promises you make to him.⁵ *It is better to say nothing than to make a promise and not keep it.*

"God's Going to Do What He Wants Anyway"

The following story is an incredible example of how God changed His mind because of human prayer. Let it give you the courage to go before the throne.

Genesis 18:20-33

> ²⁰ So the Lord told Abraham, "I have heard a great outcry from Sodom and Gomorrah, because their sin is so flagrant. ²¹ I am going down to see if their actions are as wicked as I have heard. If not, I want to know."

> ²² The other men turned and headed toward Sodom, but the Lord remained with Abraham. ²³ Abraham approached him and said, "Will you sweep away both the righteous and the wicked? ²⁴ Suppose you find fifty righteous people living there in the city—will you still sweep it away and not spare it for their sakes? ²⁵ Surely you wouldn't do such a thing, destroying the righteous along with the wicked. Why, you would be treating the righteous and the wicked exactly the same! Surely you wouldn't do that! Should not the Judge of all the earth do what is right?" ²⁶ And the Lord replied, "If I find fifty righteous people in Sodom, I will spare the entire city for their sake."

> ²⁷ Then Abraham spoke again. "Since I have begun, let me speak further to my Lord, even though I am but dust and ashes. ²⁸ Suppose there are only forty-five righteous people rather than fifty? Will you destroy the whole city for lack of five?" And the Lord said, "I will not destroy it if I find forty-five righteous people there."

> ²⁹ Then Abraham pressed his request further. "Suppose there are only forty?" And the Lord replied, "I will not destroy it for the sake of the forty."

[30] "Please don't be angry, my Lord," Abraham pleaded. "Let me speak—suppose only thirty righteous people are found?" And the Lord replied, "I will not destroy it if I find thirty."

[31] Then Abraham said, "Since I have dared to speak to the Lord, let me continue—suppose there are only twenty?" And the Lord replied, "Then I will not destroy it for the sake of the twenty."

[32] Finally, Abraham said, "Lord, please don't be angry with me if I speak one more time. Suppose only ten are found there?" And the Lord replied, "Then I will not destroy it for the sake of the ten." [33] When the Lord had finished his conversation with Abraham, he went on his way, and Abraham returned to his tent.

POINTS TO PONDER:

Based on your own experiences, which one of the misconceptions stands out to you? Use your journal to write down some key points you want to remember.

PRAYER:

Elohe Chaseddi, God of Mercy, forgive me for harboring wrong ideas about You. I want to learn to pray more boldly and more powerfully. Please help me to learn what is false in my attitude about my conversations with You.

12
Bouncy House Prayers

"If you wonder if the prayers you pray are bouncing off the ceiling, you're feeling alone, I want you to know, know you are known."

– Matthew West

The misconception that "It feels like my prayers are bouncing off the ceiling" merits an entire chapter because it is so prevalent. You are not the only one who feels this way. Even the great heroes in the Bible wondered where God was hiding at times.

Psalm 13:1

O Lord, how long will you forget me? Forever?

Psalm 22:1-2

[1] My God, my God, why have you abandoned me? Why are you so far away when I groan for help? [2] Every day I call to you, my God, but you do not answer. Every night I lift my voice, but I find no relief. How long will you look the other way?

Job 23:8-9

[8] I go east, but he is not there. I go west, but I cannot find him. [9] I do not see him in the north, for he is hidden. I look to the south, but he is concealed.

However, we can't judge God's presence based on our feelings. C.S. Lewis reminds us that "God has infinite attention to spare for each one of us. You are as much alone with him as if you were the only being he had ever created."[12] Always fill your mind with the truth: your prayers are so precious that He saves them.

Revelation 5:6-8

Then I saw a Lamb that looked as if it had been slaughtered, but it was now standing between the throne and the four living beings and among the twenty-four elders. He had seven horns and seven eyes, which represent the sevenfold Spirit of God that is sent out into every part of the earth. [7] He stepped forward and took the scroll from the right hand of the one sitting on the throne. [8] And when he took the scroll, the four living beings and the twenty-four elders fell down before the Lamb. Each one had a harp, and they held *gold bowls filled with incense, which are the prayers of God's people.*

We don't need to say the right words or even have the right attitude to get God's attention. We already have it. We have immediate access!

> Psalm 34:15
>
> The eyes of the Lord watch over those who do right;
> his ears are open to their cries for help.
>
> Hebrews 4:16
>
> So let us come boldly to the throne of our gracious God. There we will receive his mercy, and we will find grace to help us when we need it most.

Imagine walking boldly into a throne room, knowing the King would willingly spend time with you. This story puts it into perspective.

> During John F. Kennedy's administration, photographers sometimes captured a winsome scene. Seated around the President's desk, cabinet members are debating matters of world consequence, such as the Cuban missile crisis. Meanwhile, a toddler, the two-year-old John-John, crawls atop the huge Presidential desk, oblivious to White House protocol and the weighty matters of state. John-John was simply visiting his daddy and sometimes to his father's delight he would wander into the Oval Office with nary a knock.[13]

From taking care of a toddler, I know that she does not need to approach me with a certain formula or the right words when she wants my attention or needs my help. All she has to do is cry "Nana," and I am ready to scoop her into my arms and listen; I am ready to meet her needs. Jesus addresses God as "Abba" in the New Testament. This indicates the close, intimate relationship He had with His Father, similar to our "Daddy." When I was a junior in high school in New Jersey, my family hosted an exchange student from Turkey. Aydin is a tall, beautiful blond, one year older than me. We are still friends. I remember her being homesick, and in the 70s, phone calls across the Atlantic were expensive. I will never forget overhearing her talking on the phone to her dad at Christmas.

She was crying, and she kept repeating "Abba, Abba." The love she had for her dad is what our Father longs to receive from you and me.

<u>Romans 8:15</u>

> So you have not received a spirit that makes you fearful slaves. Instead, you received God's Spirit when he adopted you as his own children. Now we call him, "Abba, Father."

I like the way D.L. Moody puts it: "Some people think God does not like to be troubled with our constant coming and asking. The way to trouble God is not to come at all."

Sometimes, we think God is not listening because our feelings are often so dependent on circumstances. We are issue-centered rather than God-centered. Do any of the following phrases sound familiar to you?

"I'm not getting anything out of my quiet times."

"I wish the Bible was more relevant."

"God doesn't care about my problems."

These kinds of statements treat God as a means, not an end. God may seem far away because we don't adore Him enough. The following is from a book by a Russian Orthodox Archbishop that taught me much about prayer.

> Let us think of our prayers, yours and mine; think of the warmth, the depth and intensity of your prayer when it concerns someone you love or something which matters to your life. Then your heart is open, all your inner self is recollected in the prayer. Does it mean that God matters to you? No, it does not. It simply means that the subject matter of your prayer matters to you. For when you have made your passionate, deep, intense prayer concerning the person you love or the situation that worries you, and you turn to the next item, which does not matter so much — if you suddenly grow cold, what has changed? Has God grown cold? Has He gone? No, it means that all the elation, all the intensity in your prayer was not born of God's presence, of your faith

in Him, of your longing for Him, of your awareness of Him; it was born of nothing but your concern for him or her or it, not for God. How can we feel surprised, then, that this absence of God affects us? It is we who make ourselves absent, it is we who grow cold the moment we are no longer concerned with God. Why? Because He does not matter so much.[14]

POINTS TO PONDER:

Listed here are different versions of Hebrews 4:16 which was quoted earlier in this book. Let the truth of how much our Lord wants to be with you soak deeply into your spirit.

> So whenever we are in need, we should come bravely before the throne of our merciful God. There we will be treated with undeserved kindness, and we will find help. (CEV)

> Therefore let us [with privilege] approach the throne of grace [that is, the throne of God's gracious favor] with confidence *and* without fear, so that we may receive mercy [for our failures] and find [His amazing] grace to help in time of need [an appropriate blessing, coming just at the right moment]. (Amplified Bible)

> Now that we know what we have—Jesus, this great High Priest with ready access to God—let's not let it slip through our fingers. We don't have a priest who is out of touch with our reality. He's been through weakness and testing, experienced it all—all but the sin. So let's walk right up to him and get what he is so ready to give. Take the mercy, accept the help. (The Message)

PRAYER:

Abba, Abba, I repent for all the times I have wondered whether You are listening. I sit here before You now in faith that You love me and are always ready to dialogue.

13
Prayer Hindrances

"The irony is that while God doesn't need us, but still wants us, we desperately need God but don't really want Him most of the time."

- Francis Chan

Hopefully, after the last chapter, we are now in a position of wanting to pray. But there still might be a few obstacles in our way. Let's examine some common hurdles.

Lack of Discipline

Our prayer lives will never be what God intends if we don't put some muscle behind our goals. I'm sure everyone handles discipline differently. Maybe some of you are great at making lists and sticking to them. Others might be talented at scheduling a time with God that they write on the calendar. Now, I know better than I did 40 years ago that God loves me unconditionally. I am not less precious to Him for not getting up at 4 a.m. and pray on my knees on a cold floor for two hours before anyone else is awake. I am pretty sure that some version of this vision of "spiritual" exists deep within most of us.

I fluctuate between trying to be disciplined and "living in the moment." But I like how Yancey explains our need for structure.

> For years I resisted a regular routine of prayer, believing that communication with God should be spontaneous and free. As a result I prayed infrequently and with little satisfaction. Eventually I learned that spontaneity often flows from discipline. Leonardo da Vinci spent ten years drawing ears, elbows, hands, and other parts of the body in many different aspects. Then one day he set aside the exercises and painted what he saw. Likewise, athletes and musicians never become great without regular practice. I found that I needed the discipline of regularity to make possible those exceptional times of free communication with God.
>
> The English word *meditate* derives from a Latin word which means "to rehearse." Virgil speaks of a shepherd boy "meditating" on his flute. Often my prayers seem like a kind of rehearsal. I go over basic notes (the Lord's Prayer), practice familiar pieces (the Psalms) and try out a few new tunes. Mainly, I show up.[15]

Lack of Zeal

Do you try to give God only bits and pieces of your time, attention, and focus? I know I do. I secretly hope that He will not just be satisfied with my quick devotional or half attentive prayer but that He is actually thrilled that I remembered to visit with Him at all. But in reality, He wants to choose where and how and when we worship. He wants to be in charge of everything about our lives. I am willing to bet that most people reading this have not arrived at the place of complete rest. We still basically do what we please and add God into our lives as an extra bonus.

Deuteronomy 12:4-11

4 "Do not worship the Lord your God in the way these pagan peoples worship their gods. 5 Rather, you must seek the Lord your God at the place of worship he himself will choose from among all the tribes—the place where his name will be honored. 6 There you will bring your burnt offerings, your sacrifices, your tithes, your sacred offerings, your offerings to fulfill a vow, your voluntary offerings, and your offerings of the firstborn animals of your herds and flocks. 7 There you and your families will feast in the presence of the Lord your God, and you will rejoice in all you have accomplished because the Lord your God has blessed you.

8 "Your *pattern of worship* will change. Today all of you are doing as you please, 9 because you have not yet arrived at the place of rest, the land the Lord your God is giving you as your special possession. 10 But you will soon cross the Jordan River and live in the land the Lord your God is giving you. When he gives you rest from all your enemies and you're living safely in the land, 11 you must bring everything I command you—your burnt offerings, your sacrifices, your tithes, your sacred offerings, and your offerings to fulfill a vow—to the designated place of worship, the place the Lord your God chooses for his name to be honored.

Now, let's begin developing a desire to change our "pattern of worship." I am currently trying to change my pattern of worship by either 1) praying out loud or 2) listening to praise music in the car rather than my standard radio stations.

Distractions

Whether it is roommates or television or your phone, it is so easy to get settled in for some quality time with the Lord when, *poof*, your mind is a million miles away. Try changing your posture if you are sleepy, or praying aloud, or singing a Psalm, or writing out your prayers. Remind yourself of your priorities.

Philippians 3:7-8

> [7] I once thought these things were valuable, but now I consider them worthless because of what Christ has done. [8] Yes, everything else is worthless when compared with the infinite value of knowing Christ Jesus my Lord. For his sake I have discarded everything else, counting it all as garbage, so that I could gain Christ [9] and become one with him.

Once you have cleared your brain, follow this advice:

> ... choose such words of prayer as are completely true to what you are, words which you are not ashamed of, which express you adequately and are worthy of you—and then offer them to God with all the intelligence of which you are capable.... Ask yourself also how much they touch your heart, to what extent you are capable of concentrating your mind on them—for if you cannot be attentive to the words you say, why should God? How can He receive them as an expression of love if you do not put your heart into them, if you have only put in a certain amount of courtesy together with a certain amount of absent-mindedness?[16]

Another way to look at distractions is to embrace them.

> People often complain of "distractions" during prayer. Their mind goes wandering off on to other things. This is nearly always due to praying for something you do not really much want; you just think it would be proper and respectable and "religious" to want it. So you pray high-mindedly for big but distance things like peace in Northern Ireland or you pray that your aunt will get better from the flu—when in fact you do not much care about these things; perhaps you ought to but you don't. And so your prayer is rapidly invaded by distractions arising from what you really do want—promotion at work, let us say. Distractions are nearly always your real wants breaking in on your prayer for edifying but bogus wants. If you are distracted, trace your distraction back to the real desires it comes from and

pray about these. When you are praying for what you really want you will not be distracted. People on sinking ships do not complain of distractions during their prayer.[17]

Sin

This may seem too obvious to mention, but if you or I have a habitual sin that we are holding onto, our prayer life will suffer.

Isaiah 59:1-2

Listen! The Lord's arm is not too weak to save you, nor is his ear too deaf to hear you call. It's your sins that have cut you off from God. Because of your sins, he has turned away and will not listen anymore.

I Peter 3:7

In the same way, you husbands must give honor to your wives. Treat your wife with understanding as you live together. She may be weaker than you are, but she is your equal partner in God's gift of new life. Treat her as you should *so your prayers will not be hindered*.

Proverbs 28:9

God detests the prayers of a person who ignores the law.

POINTS TO PONDER:

In your journal, record one of your greatest distractions and write down a method for counteracting it.

PRAYER:

I don't want to be hindered by anything when I talk with You, Lord. Please help me approach You often and with confidence.

14
DOUBT

"Doubt. . . is indecision between belief and disbelief. . .Doubt can result in delaying or rejecting relevant action out of concern for mistakes or missed opportunities."

- WIKIPEDIA

Our actions speak louder than words when it comes to trusting God.

> The disciples were caught in the middle of a storm on the sea. Jesus rebuked them, not for their human tendency to fear, but for their failure to recognize His presence, protection, and power (Matt. 8:23-27). In this case their actions revealed their unbelief rather than their faith. When the storms of life overtake us as this storm overtook the disciples, we often respond as if God does not exist or does not care.[18]

Read the following story. What is Abram's complaint? (I don't know about you, but I am often amazed by how smart-alecky the heroes in the Bible could be and get away with it. It just proves how much the Lord desires honest communication with His children.)

> Genesis 15:1-6
>
> [1] Some time later, the Lord spoke to Abram in a vision and said to him, "Do not be afraid, Abram, for I will protect you, and your reward will be great."
>
> [2] But Abram replied, "O Sovereign Lord, what good are all your blessings when I don't even have a son? Since you've given me no children, Eliezer of Damascus, a servant in my household, will inherit all my wealth. [3] You have given me no descendants of my own, so one of my servants will be my heir."
>
> [4] Then the Lord said to him, "No, your servant will not be your heir, for you will have a son of your own who will be your heir." [5] Then the Lord took Abram outside and said to him, "Look up into the sky and count the stars if you can. That's how many descendants you will have!"
>
> [6] And Abram believed the Lord, and the Lord counted him as righteous because of his faith.

Maybe your version would be something like this: "Thanks for the good job You gave me, Lord, but without a husband, it's sort of pointless. There's no point in saving money for a future when I'm just going to be alone anyway."

God promised Abram a son, and Abram believed Him! Good for him, right? But it took TWENTY-FIVE years for a baby to appear. Abram was 75 when the Lord told him in Genesis 12 that he would be the father of many nations. The Scripture above showing his frustration is during the waiting period. Genesis 16 tells the well-known story of Sarai and Abram taking matters into their own hands after despairing that God's promise would never materialize. Abram (now Abraham) is 100 and Sarai (Sarah) is 90 years old when Isaac is finally born. Have you been waiting for that long?

Do you remember the next trauma in Isaac's young life? God asks Isaac's dad to sacrifice his beloved son. When I was 38, I felt like I had already dealt with the issue of not being married and that I was semi-sort-of-okay with God's timing for having a man in my life. But I was approaching 40, and my hunger for a baby was approaching an all-time high at the same time it was getting more and more unrealistic. I don't "hear" from God very often, but that morning in church, I heard Him ask me point blank if I was willing to give up my dream of having a baby, just like Abraham was willing to let go of his son Isaac, the most special answer to his prayer.

I wondered if I was making it up. I have a tendency to be overdramatic. But moments later, my San Diego Pastor, Richard Dresselhaus, began his sermon on Abraham's willingness to sacrifice his son. That was one of the hardest days of my life, but I felt that I was at a watershed moment. C.S. Lewis says it perfectly: "We're not doubting that God will do the best for us; we're wondering how painful the best will turn out to be."

This is the entry from my journal:

> I went to the altar and cried. Just like Abraham thought his life didn't make sense as he climbed the mountain to kill his son of promise, neither does my life. I would be a really great mom. Why doesn't God see that? But there was a ram in the thicket for Abraham and there will be for me too— God will provide for my needs, and this will make sense one day.

Remember that through our involvement with a pro-life group, Bob and I ended up as part-time caregivers for a newborn, who is now a toddler. God honored my trust in Him by allowing me to be not only a Nana to nine grandchildren but to even have a baby in my home. I am in my 60s and getting those diaper years a little late, but what an enormous joy that this child is in our lives. The Lord is amazing beyond words.

He also understands our human tendency to doubt. Gideon obeyed the Lord and reduced his army to a measly 300 soldiers. Read how our Lord is patient with Gideon's hesitation about the upcoming battle.

<u>Judges 7:9-15 (The Message)</u>

That night, God told Gideon: "Get up and go down to the camp. I've given it to you. If you have any doubts about going down, go down with Purah your armor bearer; when you hear what they're saying, you'll be bold and confident." He and his armor bearer Purah went down near the place where sentries were posted. Midian and Amalek, all the easterners, were spread out on the plain like a swarm of locusts. And their camels! Past counting, like grains of sand on the seashore!

[13] Gideon arrived just in time to hear a man tell his friend a dream. He said, "I had this dream: A loaf of barley bread tumbled into the Midianite camp. It came to the tent and hit it so hard it collapsed. The tent fell!"

[14] His friend said, "This has to be the sword of Gideon son of Joash, the Israelite! God has turned Midian—the whole camp!—over to him."

[15] When Gideon heard the telling of the dream and its interpretation, he went to his knees before God in prayer. Then he went back to the Israelite camp and said, "Get up and get going! God has just given us the Midianite army!"

We won't always be as lucky as Gideon was to get a clear, reassuring message directly from heaven. When we are faced with really hard circumstances, we have a choice in how we respond. I pray you are allowing your singleness, or whatever life situation is confronting you at the moment, to be a workshop for God.

> Satan wants your pain to get you offended at God; God wants your pain to press you into His face with a fervency that will produce change in you. The very thing that Satan wants to use to cause you to pull away from God, God will use to cause you to get to know Him more intimately than ever before.[19]

Imagine, just for a moment, that you actually completely believed that God would do whatever you asked. Can you think of any reason you wouldn't start praying immediately? Remember the story of the little girl who carried an umbrella to church during the drought because the pastor prayed for rain? D.L. Moody says, "If you pray for bread and bring no basket to carry it, you prove the doubting spirit, which may be the only hindrance to the boon you ask."

I don't think I need to remind you that we are talking about praying for things that are in His heart. I think you know that this is not about snapping your fingers and demanding a million dollars. I believe that we don't trust God to answer because we don't feel truly connected to Him. Most of us have a hard time spending ten minutes waiting for Him in silence. Yet scripture clearly says that if we seek, we will find. I challenge you to pray bigger and bolder. Pray as if God will answer you. Be persistent, pray often, and wait for His reply.

<u>Psalm 5:3</u>

> Listen to my voice in the morning, Lord
> Each morning I bring my requests to you and wait expectantly.

I, too, am guilty of not praying in this way, as so many people are. We pray and then forget about it. We pray because we should, but honestly, we often don't expect an answer. How sad this must make Father God that His children trust Him so little.

You know the story of Mary and Martha. Martha gets a bad reputation for being busy in the kitchen. I always feel sorry for her because the kitchen is my comfort zone too when I have company. But I think her real mistake is doubting Jesus' good intentions. She accuses Him of being unfair (Luke 10:40). Yet not even listening as Mary did is enough. The Pharisees listened to Jesus and thought He was a possessed demon. We must listen with faith.

POINTS TO PONDER:

God loves us and is patient, but His heart longs for us to trust Him more and more. Read this familiar passage. Then, close your eyes and imagine being on that boat. Spend a few moments immersing yourself in the scene, and then journal what all of your five senses are reporting. What do the waves sound like? What does the water that is sprayed by the wind taste like? What does the small boat feel like as it bounces on the lake?

Now imagine being Peter. What do you want to say to your Master?

Matthew 14:28-31

[28] Then Peter called to him, "Lord, if it's really you, tell me to come to you, walking on the water."

[29] "Yes, come," Jesus said.

So Peter went over the side of the boat and walked on the water toward Jesus. 30 But when he saw the strong wind and the waves, he was terrified and began to sink. "Save me, Lord!" he shouted.

[31] Jesus immediately reached out and grabbed him. "You have so little faith," Jesus said. "Why did you doubt me?"

PRAYER:

I confess that I am still plagued by doubts, my Savior. I want to trust You absolutely. Deal with me mercifully and guide me to a place of greater security.

15
INTERCESSION

"Faith in a prayer-hearing God will make a prayer-loving Christian."

- ANDREW MURRAY

If you are in a season of doubt, start praying for others, and keep a journal of how God answers you. It is a good method to ensure that you are pushing through to the throne.

> God gave us intercessory prayer so we could partner with Him in transforming society, saving the lost, and establishing His Kingdom. To be sure, God is perfectly capable of doing these things without us. He is all-wise, full of love, and almighty. In His wisdom He always knows what is best. In His love He always chooses what is best. And in His power He is able to do what is best. He doesn't need us. Nevertheless, in His sovereign good pleasure, He has chosen to involve us, through our prayers, in accomplishing His will. Our intercessory prayers are important to God; and they should also be important to us.[20]

Who should we pray for? The list is exhaustive. Read the following verses, and write down the category of people being discussed. Be creative. At different stages in my life, I've prayed for various groups on different days. For example, Monday I pray for my family, Tuesday I pray for government, etc. Or if you still get a newspaper, try praying through the articles. Or stop and pray as you scroll through Facebook. You'll find that praying for a different set of people other than the same old ones you always pray for may invigorate your communication with the Almighty.

<u>Psalm 106:19-23</u>

[19] The people made a calf at Mount Sinai;
they bowed before an image made of gold.
[20] They traded their glorious God
for a statue of a grass-eating bull.
[21] They forgot God, their savior,
who had done such great things in Egypt—
[22] such wonderful things in the land of Ham,
such awesome deeds at the Red Sea.
[23] So he declared he would destroy them.
But Moses, his chosen one, stepped between the Lord and the people.
He begged him to turn from his anger and not destroy them.

Daniel 9:2-6

During the first year of his reign, I, Daniel, learned from reading the word of the Lord, as revealed to Jeremiah the prophet, that Jerusalem must lie desolate for seventy years. [3] So I turned to the Lord God and pleaded with him in prayer and fasting. I also wore rough burlap and sprinkled myself with ashes.
[4] I prayed to the Lord my God and confessed:
"O Lord, you are a great and awesome God! You always fulfill your covenant and keep your promises of unfailing love to those who love you and obey your commands. [5] But we have sinned and done wrong. We have rebelled against you and scorned your commands and regulations. [6] We have refused to listen to your servants the prophets, who spoke on your authority to our kings and princes and ancestors and to all the people of the land.

1 Timothy 2:1-2

I urge you, first of all, to pray for all people. Ask God to help them; intercede on their behalf, and give thanks for them. [2] Pray this way for kings and all who are in authority so that we can live peaceful and quiet lives marked by godliness and dignity.

John 17:20-21

[20] I am praying not only for these disciples but also for all who will ever believe in me through their message. [21] I pray that they will all be one, just as you and I are one—as you are in me, Father, and I am in you. And may they be in us so that the world will believe you sent me.

Luke 22:31-32

[31] "Simon, Simon, Satan has asked to sift each of you like wheat. [32] But I have pleaded in prayer for you, Simon, that your faith should not fail. So when you have repented and turned to me again, strengthen your brothers."

Acts 12:5

But while Peter was in prison, the church prayed very earnestly for him.

James 5:13-16

¹³ Are any of you suffering hardships? You should pray. Are any of you happy? You should sing praises. ¹⁴ Are any of you sick? You should call for the elders of the church to come and pray over you, anointing you with oil in the name of the Lord. ¹⁵ Such a prayer offered in faith will heal the sick, and the Lord will make you well. And if you have committed any sins, you will be forgiven.

¹⁶ Confess your sins to each other and pray for each other so that you may be healed. The earnest prayer of a righteous person has great power and produces wonderful results.

Luke 23:32-34

³² Two others, both criminals, were led out to be executed with him. ³³ When they came to a place called The Skull, they nailed him to the cross. And the criminals were also crucified—one on his right and one on his left.

³⁴ Jesus said, "Father, forgive them, for they don't know what they are doing." And the soldiers gambled for his clothes by throwing dice.

Ephesians 6:18-19

¹⁸ Pray in the Spirit at all times and on every occasion. Stay alert and be persistent in your prayers for all believers everywhere.

¹⁹ And pray for me, too. Ask God to give me the right words so I can boldly explain God's mysterious plan that the Good News is for Jews and Gentiles alike.

Mark 10:13-16

¹³ One day some parents brought their children to Jesus so he could touch and bless them. But the disciples scolded the parents for bothering him.

¹⁴ When Jesus saw what was happening, he was angry with his disciples. He said to them, "Let the children come to me. Don't stop them! For the Kingdom of God belongs to those who are like these children. ¹⁵ I tell you the truth, anyone

who doesn't receive the Kingdom of God like a child will never enter it." ¹⁶ Then he took the children in his arms and placed his hands on their heads and blessed them.

Psalm 122:6-7

⁶ Pray for peace in Jerusalem.
May all who love this city prosper.
⁷ O Jerusalem, may there be peace within your walls
  and prosperity in your palaces.

1 John 5:16a

If you see a fellow believer sinning in a way that does not lead to death, you should pray, and God will give that person life.

Ps 106	
1 Tim 2	
John 17	
Luke 22	
Acts 12	Prisoners
James 5	
Luke 23	
Eph. 6	
Mark 10	Children
Ps 122	
1 John 5	

You've probably heard: God is on the lookout for someone to stand in the gap.

Ezekiel 22:30-31

"I looked for someone who might rebuild the wall of righteousness that guards the land. I searched for someone to stand in the gap in the wall so I wouldn't have to destroy the land, but I found no one. 31 So now I will pour out my fury on them, consuming them with the fire of my anger. I will heap on their heads the full penalty for all their sins. I, the Sovereign Lord, have spoken!"

If you are like me, you may shy away from such an enormous responsibility. Maybe you aren't called to save an entire nation, but consider the impact that your prayer in the middle of the night may have to help a depressed friend. Your persistence in praying for a buddy with cancer may be just the encouragement she needs to stand firm in her faith. My husband and I went through a rough year. My stepmother, mother, and father all died within nine weeks of each other. Several months later, our 13-year old grandson took his own life. Our world was rocked; we were off balance. Our faith was shaken. I am completely and utterly convinced that it was the enormous prayer support from hundreds of people around the world (through the power of social media and missionary connections) that kept our sanity intact and our walk with Jesus unharmed. The first step in intercession has to be believing that your prayers make a difference.

Interceding will also change you:

We the "body of Christ" have formed a partnership to dispense God's love and grace to others. As we experience that grace, inevitably we want to share it with others. Love does not come naturally to me, I must say. I need prayer in order to place myself within the force field of God's love, allowing God to fill me with compassion that I cannot muster on my own.

This way of viewing the world changes how I pray for others. Crudely put, I once envisioned intercession as bringing requests to God that God may not have thought of, then talking God into granting them. Now I see intercession as an increase in *my* awareness. When I pray for another person, I am praying for God to open my eyes so that I can see that person as God does, and then enter into the stream of love that God already directs towards that person.

Something happens when I pray for others in this way. Bringing them into God's presence changes my attitude toward them and ultimately affects our relationship.[21]

While you are working on the skill of intercession, don't forget that you are constantly being held up in prayer by the Trinity.

Romans 8:26-27, 34 (The Passion Translation)

²⁶ And in a similar way, the Holy Spirit takes hold of us in our human frailty to empower us in our weakness. For example, at times we don't even know how to pray, or know the best things to ask for. But the Holy Spirit rises up within us to super-intercede on our behalf, pleading to God with emotional sighs too deep for words.

²⁷ God, the searcher of the heart, knows fully our longings, yet he also understands the desires of the Spirit, because the Holy Spirit passionately pleads before God for us, his holy ones, in perfect harmony with God's plan and our destiny.

³⁴ Who then is left to condemn us? Certainly not Jesus, the Anointed One! For he gave his life for us, and even more than that, he has conquered death and is now risen, exalted, and enthroned by God at his right hand. So how could he possibly condemn us since he is continually praying *for our triumph?*

The fact that Jesus is praying for me just floats my boat!

POINTS TO PONDER:

Look back on the list you created of types of people for whom to pray. Who is often on your prayer list and who is seldom considered?

PRAYER:

Lord Jesus, forgive me for being selfish even in my intercession. It is so much easier to think of just my needs or those of my friends and family, and I forget that You have called us beyond our borders. Give me an increased awareness of the power of prayer and of those who are in need.

16
Unanswered Prayer

"The only times my prayers are never answered is on the golf course."

- Billy Graham

Before we delve into this topic, are you positive that God hasn't answered your prayers?

> Our problem is that we pray and then never relate anything that happens to our praying. After you pray, the greatest single thing you need to do is turn on your spiritual concentration. When you pray in a direction immediately anticipate the activity of God in answer to your prayer. I find this all the way through the Scripture: when God's people prayed, He responded.
>
> Here's what happens if you pray and then forget about what you have prayed. Things start to happen during the day that are not normal for your day. You see them all as distractions and try to get rid of them. You fail to connect them with what you have just prayed.
>
> When I pray, I immediately begin to watch for what happens next. I prepare to make adjustments to what begins to happen in my life. When I pray, it never crosses my mind that God is not going to answer. Expect God to answer your prayers but stick around for the answer. His timing is always right and best.[22]

<u>Don't Give Up</u>

Skim the story just before the one below. Jesus must have been exhausted after casting out a legion of demons. Now, He is now on His way to minister to yet another difficult situation.

> <u>Luke 8:40-48</u>
>
> [40] On the other side of the lake the crowds welcomed Jesus, because they had been waiting for him. [41] Then a man named Jairus, a leader of the local synagogue, came and fell at Jesus' feet, pleading with him to come home with him. [42] His only daughter, who was about twelve years old, was dying.
>
> As Jesus went with him, he was surrounded by the crowds. [43] A woman in the crowd had suffered for twelve years with constant bleeding, and she could find no cure. [44] Coming up behind Jesus, she touched the fringe of his robe. Immediately, the bleeding stopped.

⁴⁵ "Who touched me?" Jesus asked.

Everyone denied it, and Peter said, "Master, this whole crowd is pressing up against you."

⁴⁶ But Jesus said, "Someone deliberately touched me, for I felt healing power go out from me." ⁴⁷ When the woman realized that she could not stay hidden, she began to tremble and fell to her knees in front of him. The whole crowd heard her explain why she had touched him and that she had been immediately healed. ⁴⁸ "Daughter," he said to her, "your faith has made you well. Go in peace."

Reflect on a time when you were in a crowded place. What did you like and dislike about being in a crowd?

Close your eyes and think of this scene using all of your five senses. What do you hear? What smells might there be? What textures do you feel? What does the scenery look like?

Despite all these factors, Jesus stops at the touch of one woman. What do you think made her stand out?

Put yourself in the woman's place. How might she have felt after suffering for 12 years?

Imagine the countless doctors' visits, the sleepless nights, the pain, and hopelessness. Add to that the trauma of being scorned by her neighbors for being unclean.

Are you discouraged by unanswered prayers? When my stepmother Jan was young, she lost her sister Sandy to cancer. Sandy was a young mom, and Jan often prayed at her bedside like a good Catholic girl, pleading with God to spare her. When Sandy died, something in Jan clicked off. She allowed her connection with the Lord to close. It is very hard to learn to pray with complete faith and yet still allow God to be God ultimately.

Perhaps your unanswered prayer has to do with not being married yet, or not being financially stable, or troubles at work. In addition to wanting to find a man, I also felt that my ministry was fruitless. I spent four years as a missionary, and I didn't receive the human recognition that I thought I deserved. Once a month, we had a meeting for small group leaders. Awards were given to individuals who achieved specific goals like having a certain number of their group members be baptized or inviting their friends to church, etc. In four years, I never got to go the front of the room to receive an award. I was very discouraged.

Like this suffering woman, the choice in times of frustration is to either give up or to press forward. She wanted to touch Jesus badly enough that she ignored those who were surely taunting her in the crowd. She was willing to do what it took to reach Him. You and I have the same choice every day. Do we let our doubt prevent us from moving towards Him?

The conclusion to my story is that just before I moved from Chicago to Wisconsin, I attended my church's celebration banquet. People came from all over the city. There were people there who used to attend but had lost touch with us. To my great amazement, a handful of young women stopped by my table to say hi and to tell me what knowing me had done in their lives. Some had been good friends, while others I barely knew. But God had used something I said in each of their lives to draw them closer to Himself, without my even being aware of it. This was very humbling and a powerful reminder that His plan is far more important than any of man's rewards.

Walk Forward

The background to the following story is that the King of Aram lay siege to Samaria. Conditions became so dire that a woman even killed and ate her own son (2 Kings 6).

2 Kings 7:3-4

[3] Now there were four men with leprosy sitting at the entrance of the city gates. "Why should we sit here waiting to die?" they asked each other. [4] "We will starve if we stay here, but with the famine in the city, we will starve if we go back there. So we might as well go out and surrender to the

Aramean army. If they let us live, so much the better. But if they kill us, we would have died anyway."

Can you relate to the dilemma of these four lepers? Have you ever felt hopeless about a situation and ready to give up on God?

You know that if you retreat, you will be lost. If you stay put, you will just continue to wallow in your helplessness. Sometimes, going forward in the dark is the only option.[23] Like the woman in the previous story, these four men decided to take a step.

2 Kings 7:5-9

[5] So at twilight they set out for the camp of the Arameans. But when they came to the edge of the camp, no one was there! [6] For the Lord had caused the Aramean army to hear the clatter of speeding chariots and the galloping of horses and the sounds of a great army approaching. "The king of Israel has hired the Hittites and Egyptians to attack us!" they cried to one another. [7] So they panicked and ran into the night, abandoning their tents, horses, donkeys, and everything else, as they fled for their lives.

[8] When the men with leprosy arrived at the edge of the camp, they went into one tent after another, eating and drinking wine; and they carried off silver and gold and clothing and hid it. [9] Finally, they said to each other, "This is not right. This is a day of good news, and we aren't sharing it with anyone! If we wait until morning, some calamity will certainly fall upon us. Come on, let's go back and tell the people at the palace."

The men who dared to move forward despite their doubts ended up being richly rewarded. I can almost hear your complaints. "You don't understand my situation. It's too hard to trust God. He has let me down too often to trust Him now."

Let me tell you a story about my associate pastor Rick Petersen when I interned in San Diego. He was an amazingly charismatic and talented man of God who taught all his interns from an abundance of wisdom. Following God's call (complete with prophecies), Rick, his wife Catherine, and their three small children left San Diego for a smaller church up the coast. Several months later, Rick was killed in a small airplane crash. Cathie returned to San Diego and preached at her former church. It has been decades since this happened, but I have never forgotten her message, and it is my joy to share a paraphrased version of it with you.

> I am so tired of everyone asking me "How can you be so strong?" or telling me "I could never handle what you're going through." If that's how you feel, then why are you a Christian? Do you trust God or not? I am not any more special or different than you. God is holding me up. That's what He does. The Lord can be compared to water. As children, we get used to swimming pools, dabbing our toes in the shallow end and eventually learning to swim. Some people spend their whole life in the shallow end but be warned. Life may throw you into a stormy ocean without a minute to prepare. If that happens, your job is to keep doing what you've always done. If you remember how to stroke and how to float, the water will keep you from sinking. That's the property of water. Every day before the plane crash I read my Bible and prayed. That's my job. Nothing has changed. I am doing what I always do, and God's response is to keep me afloat. But remember this, and take it very seriously. The time to learn to swim is not when you're in a raging ocean. Practice now while the water is calm. Get to the point where reading your Bible and praying are second nature, and like swim strokes, they will be there when you need them.

No one would have blamed Cathie if she had wallowed in self-pity or backslid into unbelief. But she continued walking forward in the darkness, and God met her there. Decades later, she remains faithful and is now serving as a missionary.

POINTS TO PONDER:

I am greatly challenged by Henry Blackaby's caution that we usually forget our prayers. He advises that we should "immediately anticipate the activity of God in answer to your prayer" and "begin to watch for what happens next." I challenge you to keep a record of intercessory prayers and begin to be more diligent in noticing how God responds.

PRAYER:

O, Faithful God! You have told us time and again how You long to meet our needs. Give me eyes that see You working.

17
Pity Party

"Everybody thinks of changing humanity and nobody thinks of changing himself."

- Leo Tolstoy

Have you ever seen a small child having a hissy fit at an older sibling's birthday party because they weren't getting any presents? With deep regret, I remember an incident when I was about 10. For several years, my family housed a little African-American boy and girl as part of a program called Fresh Air. The two were unrelated. Shauntel (my age) and Bobby (my brother's age) came from Harlem to our much ritzier, white suburb in New Jersey. The program lasted for two weeks each summer, but my mom extended it to Christmas and Easter, etc. There are obviously all sorts of problems inherent in this arrangement, but her heart was in the right place. In any case, one Christmas my mother asked me to save some of my gifts to open later as Shauntel would not have as many. Oh, no! You were not going to mess with my Christmas!

Sometimes I think that God still wants to lean down and take my face in His hands and say, "Hey, it isn't all about you today!"

I remember one Valentine's Day party I threw for my singles' group when (surprise!) none of the guys showed up. The women ended up whining loud all night. It was a "poor me" fest that was stunning in its ferocity. I remember thinking, "If I were a man, I wouldn't want to date any of these women" because their attitudes STUNK.

My current pastor, Randy Simonson, puts it very succinctly. "Go down to Lowes, get yourself a ladder, and get over it!" He also would tell you that joy is the best antidote to a bad attitude. Joy is a fruit of the spirit. If you are a believer, fruit is growing inside of you. You shouldn't have to go hunting for joy.

Read the following verses and fill in the chart comparing the attitudes of a sinful person to the attitudes of those led by the Holy Spirit.

<u>Romans 8:5-6</u>

[5]Those who are dominated by the sinful nature think about sinful things, but those who are controlled by the Holy Spirit think about things that please the Spirit. [6] So letting your sinful nature control your mind leads to death. But letting the Spirit control your mind leads to life and peace.

Galatians 6:7-10

⁷ Don't be misled—you cannot mock the justice of God. You will always harvest what you plant. ⁸ Those who live only to satisfy their own sinful nature will harvest decay and death from that sinful nature. But those who live to please the Spirit will harvest everlasting life from the Spirit. ⁹ So let's not get tired of doing what is good. At just the right time we will reap a harvest of blessing if we don't give up. ¹⁰ Therefore, whenever we have the opportunity, we should do good to everyone—especially to those in the family of faith.

1 Peter 3:8-9

⁸ Finally, all of you should be of one mind. Sympathize with each other. Love each other as brothers and sisters. Be tender hearted and keep a humble attitude. ⁹ Don't repay evil for evil. Don't retaliate with insults when people insult you. Instead, pay them back with a blessing. That is what God has called you to do, and he will grant you his blessing.

	Attitudes of Sinful	**Attitudes of Spirit Led**
Rom		
Gal	Mocking God Harvesting decay and death	
1 Pet		Tender-hearted Humble Respond to insults with blessings

My Chicago pastor from New Life, Mark Jobe, told a story once about a man whose kids played a prank on him by spreading Gorgonzola cheese under his nose while he slept. When he woke up, he thought the room smelled, and then he thought it was the whole house. He went to get a breath of fresh air outside and concluded that the whole world smelled. This is an illustration of how we all can behave, thinking there is something wrong with the world when the real problem is right under our own nose.

This isn't rocket science, friends. If you focus on living by the Holy Spirit like the verses above, you are obviously going to be in a much better position to find the man of your dreams. It will also help you on whatever path you are seeking currently.

Another reason to escape the pity party mentality is because of how others will perceive you. D.L. Moody said once that out of 100 people, one will read the Bible and 99 will read the Christian.

Elijah is one of my favorite Bible characters. It astounds me that AFTER he had an incredible victory on Mt. Carmel, he suffers from a pity party.

1 Kings 19:1-4

¹ When Ahab got home, he told Jezebel everything Elijah had done, including the way he had killed all the prophets of Baal. ² So Jezebel sent this message to Elijah: "May the gods strike me and even kill me if by this time tomorrow I have not killed you just as you killed them."

³ Elijah was afraid and fled for his life. He went to Beersheba, a town in Judah, and he left his servant there. ⁴ Then he went on alone into the wilderness, traveling all day. He sat down under a solitary broom tree and prayed that he might die. "I have had enough, Lord," he said. "Take my life, for I am no better than my ancestors who have already died."

What different emotions is Elijah feeling in this passage? How do you reconcile his current attitude with his previous victories? If I was the Lord who had just performed a super-sized miracle (If you need to, reread the account in chapter 9 of this book), I would have slapped the back of his head (think Gibbs and McGee) and rebuked him. Instead, God responds like this:

1 Kings 19:5-7

⁵ Then he lay down and slept under the broom tree. But as he was sleeping, an angel touched him and told him, "Get

up and eat!" ⁶ He looked around and there beside his head was some bread baked on hot stones and a jar of water! So he ate and drank and lay down again.

⁷ Then the angel of the Lord came again and touched him and said, "Get up and eat some more, or the journey ahead will be too much for you."

What surprises you about what God does and does not do and/or say? The Lord understands our moodiness. He knows that Elijah is a faithful servant who is having a tough time. I guess that I would be a little down too if the king had promised to kill me within 24 hours. I love how God responds practically with food and drink. He knows that life can sometimes be "too much for you." Think about friends who are either genuinely depressed or just feeling sorry for themselves. Maybe bringing them a meal would help.

1 Kings 19:8-9a

⁸ So he got up and ate and drank, and the food gave him enough strength to travel forty days and forty nights to Mount Sinai, the mountain of God. ⁹ There he came to a cave, where he spent the night.

God gave Elijah enough food to last for a 40-day fast as he walked over 200 miles to Mt Sinai. Why do you think he headed there? Where do you go when you need answers or encouragement?

I Kings 19:9b-18

⁹ᵇ But the Lord said to him, "What are you doing here, Elijah?"

¹⁰ Elijah replied, "I have zealously served the Lord God Almighty. But the people of Israel have broken their covenant with you, torn down your altars, and killed every one of your prophets. I am the only one left, and now they are trying to kill me, too."

¹¹ "Go out and stand before me on the mountain," the Lord told him. And as Elijah stood there, the LORD passed by, and a mighty windstorm hit the mountain. It was such a terrible blast that the rocks were torn loose, but the Lord was not in

the wind. After the wind there was an earthquake, but the Lord was not in the earthquake. ¹² And after the earthquake there was a fire, but the Lord was not in the fire. And after the fire there was the sound of a gentle whisper. ¹³ When Elijah heard it, he wrapped his face in his cloak and went out and stood at the entrance of the cave.

And a voice said, "What are you doing here, Elijah?"

¹⁴ He replied again, "I have zealously served the Lord God Almighty. But the people of Israel have broken their covenant with you, torn down your altars, and killed every one of your prophets. I am the only one left, and now they are trying to kill me, too."

¹⁵ Then the Lord told him, "Go back the same way you came, and travel to the wilderness of Damascus. When you arrive there, anoint Hazael to be king of Aram. ¹⁶ Then anoint Jehu grandson of Nimshi to be king of Israel, and anoint Elisha son of Shaphat from the town of Abel-meholah to replace you as my prophet. ¹⁷ Anyone who escapes from Hazael will be killed by Jehu, and those who escape Jehu will be killed by Elisha! ¹⁸ Yet I will preserve 7,000 others in Israel who have never bowed down to Baal or kissed him!"

What does the Lord ask Elijah twice? What tone of voice do you think He used? Did His voice change the second time?

Read Elijah's first answer (v 10) out loud with the kind of attitude you think he had.

Do you think Elijah's attitude had changed by the second time he answered God? Why or why not?

What do you think God felt about Elijah's answer? What new directions does He give and how do these directions answer Elijah?

POINTS TO PONDER:

What have you learned in this chapter that may help you the next time you feel hopeless or abandoned?

PRAYER:

Jesus, You are not just the Almighty God, You are my friend. Thank you for not criticizing me when I have a bad attitude but for providing me a way to overcome difficulties in my life.

18
Perseverance

"To climb steep hills requires
a slow pace at first."

- William Shakespeare

So, you've got your prayer life sorted out, you are trying to focus on God's character, but you still face a long road. Sometimes there is no answer except to keep putting one foot forward. You never know when God will show up.

As you read the passage below, consider what Elisha was doing when he received his calling. Do you think he expected this to happen at that moment? How does this change the way you might think about each day you face?

I Kings 19:19-21

[19] So Elijah went and found Elisha son of Shaphat plowing a field. There were twelve teams of oxen in the field, and Elisha was plowing with the twelfth team. Elijah went over to him and threw his cloak across his shoulders and then walked away. [20] Elisha left the oxen standing there, ran after Elijah, and said to him, "First let me go and kiss my father and mother good-bye, and then I will go with you!"

Elijah replied, "Go on back, but think about what I have done to you."

[21] So Elisha returned to his oxen and slaughtered them. He used the wood from the plow to build a fire to roast their flesh. He passed around the meat to the townspeople, and they all ate. Then he went with Elijah as his assistant.

Throwing the cloak over Elisha's shoulders was, according to Matthew Henry's commentary, "an investiture with the prophetic office. It is in this way that the Brahmins, the Persian Sufis, and other priestly or sacred characters in the East are appointed—a mantle being, by some eminent priest, thrown across their shoulders. Elisha had probably been educated in the schools of the prophets."

Elijah was obeying what God told Him in the cave. What might be the consequences in someone else's life if we don't listen to that small voice? This is a sobering thought, isn't it? We may be stalling another woman's growth because we did not heed the call to somehow speak into her life.

Elisha was probably a man of some wealth, considering that he owed twelve teams of oxen. How can you tell that he is determined to follow in the prophet's footsteps?

How has Elijah changed since the beginning of I Kings 19? How important is Elisha in this transformation?

II Kings 2:1-6

¹ When the Lord was about to take Elijah up to heaven in a whirlwind, Elijah and Elisha were traveling from Gilgal.

² And Elijah said to Elisha, "Stay here, for the Lord has told me to go to Bethel."

But Elisha replied, "As surely as the Lord lives and you yourself live, I will never leave you!" So they went down together to Bethel.

³ The group of prophets from Bethel came to Elisha and asked him, "Did you know that the Lord is going to take your master away from you today?"

"Of course I know," Elisha answered. "But be quiet about it."

⁴ Then Elijah said to Elisha, "Stay here, for the Lord has told me to go to Jericho."

But Elisha replied again, "As surely as the Lord lives and you yourself live, I will never leave you." So they went on together to Jericho.

⁵ Then the group of prophets from Jericho came to Elisha and asked him, "Did you know that the Lord is going to take your master away from you today?"

"Of course I know," Elisha answered. "But be quiet about it."

⁶ Then Elijah said to Elisha, "Stay here, for the Lord has told me to go to the Jordan River."

But again Elisha replied, "As surely as the Lord lives and you yourself live, I will never leave you." So they went on together.

What did Elijah and Elisha say back and forth to each other three times? What is Elijah's motivation to tell Elisha to stay? What do Elisha's responses say about his character?

II Kings 2:7-14

⁷ Fifty men from the group of prophets also went and watched from a distance as Elijah and Elisha stopped beside the Jordan River.

⁸ Then Elijah folded his cloak together and struck the water with it. The river divided, and the two of them went across on dry ground!

⁹ When they came to the other side, Elijah said to Elisha, "Tell me what I can do for you before I am taken away."

And Elisha replied, "Please let me inherit a double share of your spirit and become your successor."

¹⁰ "You have asked a difficult thing," Elijah replied. "If you see me when I am taken from you, then you will get your request. But if not, then you won't."

¹¹ As they were walking along and talking, suddenly a chariot of fire appeared, drawn by horses of fire. It drove between the two men, separating them, and Elijah was carried by a whirlwind into heaven.

¹² Elisha saw it and cried out, "My father! My father! I see the chariots and charioteers of Israel!" And as they disappeared from sight, Elisha tore his clothes in distress.

¹³ Elisha picked up Elijah's cloak, which had fallen when he was taken up. Then Elisha returned to the bank of the Jordan River.

¹⁴ He struck the water with Elijah's cloak and cried out, "Where is the Lord, the God of Elijah?" Then the river divided, and Elisha went across.

Elisha wanted to serve God so much that he asked for a double portion of Elijah's spirit to serve Him. He probably saw himself as Elijah's spiritual son and was following Deuteronomy 21:17 ("He must recognize the rights of his oldest son . . . by giving him a double portion"). What do you think God thought of this request? I believe that the Lord loves it when His children are greedy for Him. Whatever level of authority you are operating at now can be increased. Perhaps it is time you sought a promotion to serve Him better. Have you ever had a desire to do something for the Lord? Maybe you wanted to start teaching Sunday School or begin a women's ministry or write a song? Did you follow through? What sort of things stood in your way? If you can easily be talked out of your calling then it might not be authentic.

Why do you think Elijah told Elisha, "if you see me when I am taken from you, then you will get your request"?

POINTS TO PONDER:

Is anyone following in your footsteps? Is there a skill or knowledge or wisdom regarding the life of Christ that you could be passing on to a younger person?

PRAYER:

Great and Mighty God, give me a portion of Elisha's determination to follow You. Open my eyes to those who I can mentor.

19
Perseverance Part 2

"Procrastination is the bad habit of putting off until the day after tomorrow what should have been done the day before yesterday."

- Napoleon Hill

In different passages, perseverance is translated as "steadfastness," "persistence," or "endurance." That same word is used when Jesus tells his disciples that a boat should *stand ready* for him (Mark 3:9, NASB). Don't you want to be someone who stands ready for Jesus? So, how is perseverance achieved?

> Any training—physical, mental, or spiritual—is characterized at first by failure. We fail more often than we succeed. But if we persevere, we gradually see progress till we are succeeding more often than failing. This is true as we seek to put to death particular sins. At first it seems we are making no progress, so we become discouraged and think, What's the use?! I can never overcome that sin. That is exactly what Satan wants us to think. It is at this point that we must exercise perseverance. We keep wanting instant success, but holiness doesn't come that way. Our sinful habits are not broken overnight. Follow-through is required to make any change in our lives, and follow-through requires perseverance.[24]

The Bible seems to indicate that recognizing that you are in a race is a good place to start.

1 Corinthians 9:24

Don't you realize that in a **race** everyone runs, but only one person gets the prize? So run to win!

Galatians 5:7

You were running the **race** so well. Who has held you back from following the truth?

Philippians 2:16

Hold firmly to the word of life; then, on the day of Christ's return, I will be proud that I did not run the **race** in vain and that my work was not useless.

2 Timothy 4:7

I have fought the good fight, I have finished the **race**, and I have remained faithful.

There is no short cut to developing perseverance. Life is a marathon, not a sprint. And the fact that we are intent on finishing the race is of the utmost importance to God.

The Olympic games in 1968 in Mexico City were the site of an incredible story of persistence. The high altitude and scorching hot day had affected all the athletes. One runner suffered severe cramps and sustained injuries in a collision with another runner, including hurting his shoulder as well as badly cutting and dislocating his knee. The stadium was almost deserted. An hour earlier, the winners of the 26-mile marathon had crossed the finish line. As the last few spectators were walking out, a runner wearing the colors of Tanzania emerged through the stadium gate. Despite a bad limp and his bandaged leg, he summoned up the last reservoir of his endurance to finish the race. His name was John Stephen Akhwari.

When asked why he continued running despite his injuries, he said, "My country did not send me 5,000 miles to start the race; they sent me 5,000 miles to finish the race."

We can't finish the race by standing on the sidelines. We have to get in the thick of things which probably means getting a little bit dirty. Plenty of people begin a race but don't finish. They hang onto their baggage and their sins, or they take their eyes off Jesus.

Imagine a basketball team that is losing badly at half time. The coach gives them a pep talk, and they come back to win in overtime. What do you think God would say to motivate you in the locker room of your life? There will always be people or circumstances that will try to knock the ball out of your hands. Keep a tight hold on your faith. Determine today that "I won't let go no matter what." Whether you are at half time, quarter time, or almost at the finish line, know that completing the race is crucial.

The Message describes the race we are in very clearly:

Hebrews 12:1-3

Do you see what this means—all these pioneers who blazed the way, all these veterans cheering us on? It means we'd better get on with it. Strip down, start running—and never quit! No extra spiritual fat, no parasitic sins. Keep your eyes on *Jesus*, who both began and finished this race we're in. Study how he did it. Because he never lost sight of where he was headed—that exhilarating finish in and with God—he could put up with anything along the way: Cross, shame, whatever. And now he's *there*, in the place of honor, right alongside God. When you find yourselves flagging in your faith, go over that story again, item by item, that long litany of hostility he plowed through. *That* will shoot adrenaline into your souls!

Christ taught a parable with some good lessons on persistence.[25]

Luke 11:5-10

⁵Then, teaching them more about prayer, he used this story: "Suppose you went to a friend's house at midnight, wanting to borrow three loaves of bread. You say to him, ⁶'A friend of mine has just arrived for a visit, and I have nothing for him to eat.' ⁷And suppose he calls out from his bedroom, 'Don't bother me. The door is locked for the night, and my family and I are all in bed. I can't help you.' ⁸But I tell you this—though he won't do it for friendship's sake, if you keep knocking long enough, he will get up and give you whatever you need because of your shameless persistence.

⁹"And so I tell you, keep on asking, and you will receive what you ask for. Keep on seeking, and you will find. Keep on knocking, and the door will be opened to you. ¹⁰ For everyone who asks, receives. Everyone who seeks, finds. And to everyone who knocks, the door will be opened.

There was an *urgent need*. Not having bread to offer visitors was a serious lapse in hospitality in that culture. When was the last time you felt desperate enough to pray at midnight? They needed bread IMMEDIATELY. Pray when and where it is necessary.

The friend responded because of the petitioner's *shameless persistence* that got that person out of bed late at night. I have heard lots of people say "Shouldn't I just pray once? God knows what I need. I don't want to bother Him or act like I don't have faith." This story clearly says keep knocking.

The hurting friend feels impotent. "I have nothing." Realizing that *we have no power to fix the situation* causes us to cry out to God.

The friend knew where to turn. He kept banging on the door because he was confident his friend was *able to meet his need*. Maybe the sleeping neighbor was rich, or maybe he was the local baker. Either way, we too can be assured that God is always able to provide.

Don't make your prayers too small. Asking for three loaves showed some chutzpah. God created the universe; He can handle whatever you ask of Him.

"If you keep knocking long enough" an answer will come. I bet that most of us give up when we on the brink of victory. We get frustrated or tired, or we lose hope.

But what happens when, despite all the knocking in the world, the answer doesn't come? The following is a familiar story that is worth rereading.

Daniel 3:13-18

[13] Then Nebuchadnezzar flew into a rage and ordered that Shadrach, Meshach, and Abednego be brought before him. When they were brought in, [14] Nebuchadnezzar said to them, "Is it true, Shadrach, Meshach, and Abednego, that you refuse to serve my gods or to worship the gold statue I have set up? [15] I will give you one more chance to bow down and worship the statue I have made when you hear the sound of the musical instruments. But if you refuse, you will be thrown immediately into the blazing furnace. And then what god will be able to rescue you from my power?"

[16] Shadrach, Meshach, and Abednego replied, "O Nebuchadnezzar, we do not need to defend ourselves before you. [17] If we are thrown into the blazing furnace, the God whom we serve is able to save us. He will rescue us from your power, Your Majesty. [18] But even if he doesn't, we want to make it clear to you, Your Majesty, that we will never serve your gods or worship the gold statue you have set up."

That's the sweet spot where I want to live—the place where I can say "even if he doesn't" fulfill my wishes, I will serve Him.

POINTS TO PONDER:

Read a different version of the same Hebrews passage.

Hebrews 12:1-3

[1] Therefore, since we are surrounded by such a huge crowd of witnesses to the life of faith, let us strip off every weight that slows us down, especially the sin that so easily trips us up. And let us run with endurance the race God has set before us. [2] We do this by keeping our eyes on Jesus, the champion who initiates and perfects our faith. Because of the joy awaiting him, he endured the cross, disregarding its shame. Now he is seated in the place of honor beside God's throne. [3] Think of all the hostility he endured from sinful people; then you won't become weary and give up. [4] After all, you have not yet given your lives in your struggle against sin.

What weight is slowing you down? What is one thing you can do this week to keep your eyes on Jesus?

PRAYER:

Lord God, there are so many obstacles in my way as I try to run towards You. Help me to swerve around them and keep me focused on the end goal.

20
Perseverance Part 3

"If you can't fly, then run, if you can't run, then walk, if you can't walk, then crawl, but whatever you do, you have to keep moving forward"

- Martin Luther King Jr.

What kind of things tempt you to stop persevering on your journey to know God?

<u>Growing Weary</u>

The church in Ephesus gets a bad reputation for the next verse about losing their first love. But let's see why they were praised.

<u>Revelation 2:1-3 (NASV)</u>

[1] "To the angel of the church in Ephesus write:

The One who holds the seven stars in His right hand, the One who walks among the seven golden lampstands, says this:

[2] 'I know your deeds and your toil and perseverance, and that you cannot tolerate evil men, and you put to the test those who call themselves apostles, and they are not, and you found them *to be* false; [3] and you have perseverance and have endured for My name's sake and have not grown weary.

When I was 38 and leading a singles' group, I got burned out from ministry. Below is a passage from my journal.

> I'm tired and I give up—which is no doubt where God wants me anyway. I've always had a long list of how to please Him, and I'm still living that way. I'm afraid to drop any of my activities because I would feel like I wasn't being obedient to some part of His call.
>
>> Monday: weight loss group because my body is His temple
>> Tuesday: teaching my small group because I can't neglect my gift
>> Wednesday: intern team meeting and 5th/6th graders as I need to be involved in ministry outside my comfort zone and get to know non-singles
>> Thursday: playing bridge as my social contact with non-Christians which is exciting to me to have friends outside of church
>> Friday: worship night which I need to feed my soul

Plus, there are quiet times and exercise every day. Plus, I try to keep a clean house and build relationships with friends and be open to new people and spend money wisely (haha) and make sure the whole world has a happy birthday.

No wonder I was tired! Have you ever felt like this? Running and running on the treadmill of trying to please God? At that time of my life, I remember feeling like the old Ziggy cartoon where he stands on top of a mountain shaking his fist at heaven and shouting, "You expect too much from me!" I told God that I couldn't do it, that being a Christian was just too hard. Suddenly, I had a vision of a long, deep, black hole. I knew that I had a clear choice. I could either try to stay the course with Jesus in spite of all the challenges, or I could enter that hole with no light and no joy. The Lord brought the following verse to my mind, and since that time I have not looked back. I have stumbled and made many wrong turns, but I am still in the race.

<u>John 6:66-67</u>

At this point many of his disciples turned away and deserted him. Then Jesus turned to the Twelve and asked, "Are you also going to leave?"

Simon Peter replied, "Lord, to whom would we go? You have the words that give eternal life. We believe, and we know you are the Holy One of God."

Much-Afraid from *Hinds Feet on High Places* had a very similar experience.

For one black, awful moment Much-Afraid really considered the possibility of following the Shepherd no longer, of turning back. She need not go on. There was absolutely no compulsion about it... During that awful moment or two it seemed to Much-Afraid that she was actually looking into an abyss of horror, into an existence in which there was no Shepherd to follow or to trust or to love—no Shepherd at all, nothing but her own horrible self. Ever after, it seemed that she had looked straight down into Hell. [. . .]

> Much-Afraid shrieked "Shepherd! Shepherd! Help me! Where are you? Don't leave me!" Next instant she was clinging to him, trembling from head to foot, and sobbing over and over again, "You may do anything, Shepherd. You may ask anything—only don't let me turn back. O my Lord, don't let me leave you." [. . .]
>
> He lifted her up, supported her by his arm, and with his own hand wiped the tears from her cheeks and said in his strong, cheery voice, "There is no question of your turning back, Much-Afraid. No one, not even your own shrinking heart, can pluck you out my hand."[26]

A few years later in Chicago, I was still dealing with similar issues. My journal from this time says:

> God wants me to experience His love in such a real way that I won't need to seek intimacy anywhere else. I promise to love Him and stand firm even if I never have sex, never hear I love you, never am held by a man, never meet my dreams of teaching, or working full-time at a church, or have a best friend. I will love God if tragedy strikes or if I'm always poor. There is nowhere else to go.

Looking Back

Think of the well-known story of God destroying Sodom and Gomorrah. "But Lot's wife looked back as she was following behind him, and she turned into a pillar of salt" (Genesis 19:26). It was too hard for her to leave her life behind.

We have read this passage before but it is worth revisiting.

Philippians 3:12-14

[12] I don't mean to say that I have already achieved these things or that I have already reached perfection. But I press on to possess that perfection for which Christ Jesus first possessed me. [13] No, dear brothers and sisters, I have not achieved it, but I focus on this one thing: Forgetting the past and looking forward to what lies ahead, [14] I press on to reach the end of the race and receive the heavenly prize for which God, through Christ Jesus, is calling us.

We can't run the race and persevere if we are looking back with regret or doubt or worry or shame.

<u>Complacency</u>

It is obviously impossible to persevere in the race if you grow uninterested in running at all.

<u>Isaiah 30:10-11</u>

¹⁰ They tell the seers,
"Stop seeing visions!"
They tell the prophets,
"Don't tell us what is right.
Tell us nice things.
Tell us lies.
¹¹ Forget all this gloom.
Get off your narrow path.
Stop telling us about your
'Holy One of Israel.'

Read the beginning of the book of Ruth again. Think of what it took Ruth to follow Naomi on her long walk home to Bethlehem. Compare her to her sister-in-law Orpah who chose the easy route of staying in her comfort zone.

> I enjoy reading C.S. Lewis because he doesn't pull any punches.
>
> On the other hand, you must realize from the outset that the goal towards which He is beginning to guide you is absolute perfection; and no power in the whole universe, except you yourself, can prevent you from taking you to that goal. That is what you are in for. . . We may be content to remain what we call ordinary people; but He is determined to carry out a quite different plan. To shrink back from that plan is not humility; it is laziness and cowardice. To submit to it is not conceit or megalomania; it is obedience.[27]

God's Word puts it like this:

<u>Isaiah 48:17-19</u>

¹⁷ This is what the Lord says—
your Redeemer, the Holy One of Israel:

"I am the Lord your God,
who teaches you what is good for you
and leads you along the paths you should follow.
¹⁸ Oh, that you had listened to my commands! Then you would have had peace flowing like a gentle river and righteousness rolling over you like waves in the sea.
¹⁹ Your descendants would have been like the sands along the seashore—too many to count!

In the above scenario, the nation ended up at war. I don't know about you, but I would rather try to follow God then to have Him later say, "You *would have had* peace".

End Results of Perseverance

2 Timothy 4:8

And now the prize awaits me—the crown of righteousness, which the Lord, the righteous Judge, will give me on the day of his return. And the prize is not just for me but for all who eagerly look forward to his appearing.

James 1:2-4, 12 (NIV)

² Consider it pure joy, my brothers and sisters, whenever you face trials of many kinds, ³ because you know that the testing of your faith produces perseverance. ⁴ Let perseverance finish its work so that you may be mature and complete, not lacking anything.

¹² Blessed is the one who perseveres under trial because, having stood the test, that person will receive the crown of life that the Lord has promised to those who love him.

Romans 5:3-5 (NIV)

Not only so, but we also glory in our sufferings, because we know that suffering produces perseverance; perseverance, character; and character, hope. And hope does not put us to shame, because God's love has been poured out into our hearts through the Holy Spirit, who has been given to us.

Hebrews 10:35-39

³⁵ So do not throw away this confident trust in the Lord. Remember the great reward it brings you! ³⁶ Patient

endurance is what you need now, so that you will continue to do God's will. Then you will receive all that he has promised.
³⁷ "For in just a little while,
the Coming One will come and not delay.
³⁸ And my righteous ones will live by faith.
But I will take no pleasure in anyone who turns away."
³⁹ But we are not like those who turn away from God to their own destruction. We are the faithful ones, whose souls will be saved.

Pastor Mark Jobe said, "The ultimate result of giving up every time it gets tough is immaturity and lack of character and not getting all God has for you. Those times when you think you can't make it are when perseverance is being developed in you and the door to all He has for you is beginning to open."

POINTS TO PONDER:

Which section of this chapter do you relate to the most? Are you like the younger me, trapped on a treadmill of trying to do it all perfectly and yet missing intimacy with Jesus? Or are you the opposite, feeling unmotivated to make any effort? For a moment, think about the prize that awaits you, the "crown of righteousness" if you continue to persevere. What might it look like or entail?

PRAYER:

All-merciful God, I confess that there are days when I don't feel like giving You my all. I ask for Your forgiveness and for a renewed spark to keep me pushing forward.

21
Complete the Work

"The Christian shoemaker does his duty not by putting little crosses on the shoes, but by making good shoes, because God is interested in good craftsmanship."

— Martin Luther.

This is a hard passage to read but I am pretty sure you will relate.

Hosea 6:1-3

¹ Come, let us return to the Lord.
He has torn us to pieces;
now he will heal us.
He has injured us;
now he will bandage our wounds.
² In just a short time he will restore us,
so that we may live in his presence.
³ Oh, that we might know the Lord!
Let us press on to know him.
He will respond to us as surely as the arrival of dawn
or the coming of rains in early spring.

Sometimes, we experience pain or unanswered prayers or flat out disobedience where we feel torn to pieces. God rejoices in our weakness when we are so disgusted with the condition of our own soul that we are ready to come to Him with our wounds.

List all the promises in these three short verses. The order is important. It is tempting to want to "live in his presence," but the process of seeking healing is a crucial step.

Don't be a spectator to what God is doing. Press on, be involved in the work he has given you to do, and complete this work. David charged his son Solomon with the task of building the temple. David was not allowed to build it himself as he had been a warrior who had shed much blood (1 Chronicles 28:3).

1 Chronicles 28: 8-10

⁸ "So now, with God as our witness, and in the sight of all Israel—the Lord's assembly—I give you this charge. Be careful to obey all the commands of the Lord your God, so that you may continue to possess this good land and leave it to your children as a permanent inheritance.

⁹ "And Solomon, my son, learn to know the God of your ancestors intimately. Worship and serve him with your whole heart and a willing mind. For the Lord sees every heart and knows every plan and thought. If you seek him,

you will find him. But if you forsake him, he will reject you forever. ¹⁰ So take this seriously. The Lord has chosen you to build a Temple as his sanctuary. Be strong, and do the work."

Note the list of things David wants to impress on his son's heart before he gives him the enormous privilege and responsibility of building God's home.

- Obey the commands
- Learn to know God intimately
- Worship
- Serve with a whole heart
- Have a willing mind

How can you tell when you are not being whole-hearted? Is it possible to serve God without a willing mind? What ways are you seeking God?

How can you guard your heart so that you won't be tempted to forsake God?

What are you called to do that you have been neglecting? It is very easy to think, "Someday, I will do something amazing for God. When I have more money. When I have more free time. When I am married or have children or finish school." Or, or, or. Challenge yourself to keep pushing past your comfort zone. It doesn't matter how old you are or what your circumstances are. God has a plan for you right now.

Just be sure that in your push to do something for God you don't confuse obedience with earning salvation. The best analogy I ever heard about good works versus grace asks you to imagine a swimming race from California to Hawaii. Someone amazingly "good" like Mother Teresa may be out a few miles while someone who is evil (think of Hitler) is floundering in the shallow end. The good may seem to be making a lot of progress towards Hawaii (heaven) but no one is going to make that swim with their own strength.

Read the following verses carefully. Make two lists of 1) what you are asked to do and 2) what God promises.

Philippians 1:6

And I am certain that God, who began the good work within you, will continue his work until it is finally finished on the day when Christ Jesus returns.

1 Corinthians 1:8

He will keep you strong to the end so that you will be free from all blame on the day when our Lord Jesus Christ returns.

Hebrews 13:20-21

[20] Now may the God of peace—
who brought up from the dead our Lord Jesus,
the great Shepherd of the sheep,
and ratified an eternal covenant with his blood—
[21] may he equip you with all you need
for doing his will.
May he produce in you,
through the power of Jesus Christ,
every good thing that is pleasing to him.
All glory to him forever and ever! Amen.

Jude 24

Now all glory to God, who is able to keep you from falling away and will bring you with great joy into his glorious presence without a single fault.

Acts 20:24

But my life is worth nothing to me unless I use it for finishing the work assigned me by the Lord Jesus—the work of telling others the Good News about the wonderful grace of God.

2 Corinthians 8:10-12

[10] Here is my advice: It would be good for you to finish what you started a year ago. Last year you were the first who wanted to give, and you were the first to begin doing it. [11] Now you should finish what you started. Let the eagerness you showed in the beginning be matched now by your giving. Give in proportion to what you have. [12] Whatever

you give is acceptable if you give it eagerly. And give according to what you have, not what you don't have.

Ecclesiastes 9:10a (NIV)

Whatever your hand finds to do, do it with all your might.

Colossians 3:23

Whatever work you do, do it with all your heart. Do it for the Lord and not for men.

John 4:34

Then Jesus explained: "My nourishment comes from doing the will of God, who sent me, and from finishing his work.

John 17:4

I brought glory to you here on earth by completing the work you gave me to do.

2 Chronicles 15:7 (NIV)

But as for you, be strong and do not give up, for your work will be rewarded.

2 Corinthians 9:6-10

[6] Remember this—a farmer who plants only a few seeds will get a small crop. But the one who plants generously will get a generous crop. [7] You must each decide in your heart how much to give. And don't give reluctantly or in response to pressure. "For God loves a person who gives cheerfully." [8] And God will generously provide all you need. Then you will always have everything you need and plenty left over to share with others. [9] As the Scriptures say,

> "They share freely and give generously to the poor.
> Their good deeds will be remembered forever."

[10] For God is the one who provides seed for the farmer and then bread to eat. In the same way, he will provide and increase your resources and then produce a great harvest of generosity in you.

<u>1 Corinthians 15:58</u>

So then, Christian brothers, because of all this, be strong. Do not allow anyone to change your mind. Always do your work well for the Lord. You know that whatever you do for Him will not be wasted.

<u>Hebrews 6:10-12</u>

[10] God always does what is right. He will not forget the work you did to help the Christians and the work you are still doing to help them. This shows your love for Christ. [11] We want each one of you to keep on working to the end. Then what you hope for, will happen. [12] Do not be lazy. Be like those who have faith and have not given up. They will receive what God has promised them

What I need to do:

What God promises:

I almost missed out on seeing God's promises fulfilled on my mission trip to Scotland. During our training sessions, we were asked to name one thing that we wanted God to do that week that we believed was too much to ask. My request was leading someone to salvation.

We were part of the Edinburgh Art Festival where a multitude of artists, preachers, and singers, gathered in a big square and performed or spoke to the crowds. The Youth with a Mission drama team enacted a series of mimes. The rest of us were supposed to just talk to people. I made a bargain with God and told Him that for the first day I wasn't going to mention His name—just talking to strangers was hard enough, and He would have to understand that I was going to break myself in easy. (Have you ever tried to tell God how it's going to be? I wouldn't advise it.)

There was an international mix of tourists. I spoke to someone from Italy with broken English, and she loved the fact that I was from California. I was excited, thinking, "I can talk about Disneyland all day." After a few more casual conversations, two teenage girls with very strong Scottish accents approached me and asked if I was a Christian. Like Peter, I was tempted to deny it. Now, just listen to how our amazing Lord acts. Then, the girls said, "We have been wanting to become Christian but don't know how. Can you tell us?" I was stunned and scared out of my mind, but we sat on some stone steps and talked. I was trying to share the gospel, and I was talking about sin, but I could see they were not connecting. In workshops, our teachers had stressed asking the Holy Spirit for the right words to reach each person's heart. This may seem obvious in talking to teens, but I felt the Spirit tell me to say, "We all sin: it may be sleeping with your boyfriend or. . ." One girl started crying and looked at me like I was a psychic. From there, it was easy. Debbie and Patricia entered the kingdom of heaven that day. I only wish that I had gotten their addresses to stay in touch.

So, the girl who didn't believe that God would use her was the only person on the whole YWAM team who led someone to the Lord the first day of the mission. YEAH, GOD.

POINTS TO PONDER:

Which of the above promises touched you the most? Take a moment to write down the verse. Post it somewhere you will see it every day, on your fridge or bathroom mirror. Let its truth settle in your heart this week.

PRAYER:

Lord God, I want to be involved in Your work. Show me a glimpse of where I fit in Your design so that I am not just a spectator.

22
Burn Out

"The difference between a successful person and others is not a lack of strength, not a lack of knowledge, but rather a lack of will."

- Vince Lombardi

Have you ever kept going even though you knew your gas tank was on empty? Did you figure you could eke out a few more miles? The Christian life can be like that—we think we can get by on the fuel we have. But as the passage below warns us, the fire "must never go out."

Leviticus 6:8-13

8 Then the Lord said to Moses, 9 "Give Aaron and his sons the following instructions regarding the burnt offering. The burnt offering must be left on top of the altar until the next morning, and the fire on the altar must be kept burning all night. 10 In the morning, after the priest on duty has put on his official linen clothing and linen undergarments, he must clean out the ashes of the burnt offering and put them beside the altar. 11 Then he must take off these garments, change back into his regular clothes, and carry the ashes outside the camp to a place that is ceremonially clean. 12 Meanwhile, the fire on the altar must be kept burning; it must never go out. Each morning the priest will add fresh wood to the fire and arrange the burnt offering on it. He will then burn the fat of the peace offerings on it. 13 Remember, the fire must be kept burning on the altar at all times. It must never go out.

Paul wouldn't have cautioned us against burning out (or lacking in zeal) if it wasn't a common issue.

Romans 12:10-13 (The Message)

9-10 Love from the center of who you are; don't fake it. Run for dear life from evil; hold on for dear life to good. Be good friends who love deeply; practice playing second fiddle.

11-13 Don't burn out; keep yourselves fueled and aflame. Be alert servants of the Master, cheerfully expectant. Don't quit in hard times; pray all the harder. Help needy Christians; be inventive in hospitality.

2 Corinthians 11:28 (The Message)

And that's not the half of it, when you throw in the daily pressures and anxieties of all the churches.

Although it seems like the Christian life can be hard, exhaustion is not part of God's plan.

Matthew 11:28-30 (The Message)

28-30 "Are you tired? Worn out? Burned out on religion? Come to me. Get away with me and you'll recover your life. I'll show you how to take a real rest. Walk with me and work with me—watch how I do it. Learn the unforced rhythms of grace. I won't lay anything heavy or ill-fitting on you. Keep company with me and you'll learn to live freely and lightly."

1 John 5:3-4 (NASB)

³ For this is the love of God, that we keep His commandments; and His commandments are not burdensome. ⁴ For whatever is born of God overcomes the world; and this is the victory that has overcome the world—our faith.

Galatians 6:9 (NIV)

Let us not become weary in doing good, for at the proper time we will reap a harvest if we do not give up.

If you're like me, you would love to learn how to "live freely and lightly" and to be able to walk in the reality that "His commandments are not burdensome."

When we get "weary and worn out" it is easy to lag behind and leave ourselves open for an enemy attack.

Deuteronomy 25:17-19

¹⁷ Remember what the Amalekites did to you along the way when you came out of Egypt. ¹⁸ When you were weary and worn out, they met you on your journey and attacked all who were lagging behind; they had no fear of God. ¹⁹ When the Lord your God gives you rest from all the enemies around you in the land he is giving you to possess as an inheritance, you shall blot out the name of Amalek from under heaven. Do not forget!

Identify what is causing burn out. Maybe you call it something else — apathy or spiritual indifference or just feeling "blah."

Load Carrying

Some of us are so consumed by ministering to others that we can fizzle out ourselves.

Colossians 4:12

Epaphras, who is one of you and a servant of Christ Jesus, sends greetings. He is always wrestling in prayer for you, that you may stand firm in all the will of God, mature and fully assured.

Colossians 1:28 –2:1

[28] So we tell others about Christ, warning everyone and teaching everyone with all the wisdom God has given us. We want to present them to God, perfect in their relationship to Christ. [29] That's why I work and struggle so hard, depending on Christ's mighty power that works within me. I want you to know how much I have agonized for you and for the church at Laodicea, and for many other believers who have never met me personally.

The word "wrestling" in the first verse above implies heavy toil to the point that it can cause pain. In the second verse, Paul seems to be the epitome of the perfect Christian, yet even he admits to difficulties. The Expositor's Bible Commentary says that word "struggle" is literally "like a man tugging at an oar and putting all his weight into each stroke." He has to depend on "Christ's mighty power."

Galatians 6:1-5 (NIV)

[1] Brothers and sisters, if someone is caught in a sin, you who live by the Spirit should restore that person gently. But watch yourselves, or you also may be tempted. [2] Carry each other's burdens, and in this way you will fulfill the law of Christ. [3] If anyone thinks they are something when they are not, they deceive themselves. [4] Each one should test their own actions. Then they can take pride in themselves alone,

without comparing themselves to someone else, ⁵ for each one should carry their own load.

Women are especially prone to wanting to "carry each other's burdens." Isn't this Biblical? The key lies in the Greek language. The burden referred to is something that is too big for one person—perhaps a tragedy or an illness. The word "load" in verse 5, on the other hand, is more like a backpack. Each of us should carry our own load rather than dumping our stuff on our friends or family. So yes, by all means, jump in to pray and counsel and hug and hold those with burdens. But if burn out starts getting to you, maybe you are trying to carry someone else's "load."

Sometimes, no matter what we do or try, we are not successful. We can't make our loved ones listen to the gospel. We can't always convince our children to make smart choices. To date, we have housed three different young women in difficult situations. All three broke our hearts to some extent, refusing to help themselves make the necessary steps to be a productive member of society.

Even the great missionary Paul felt like a failure after trying to discipline the stubborn church in Corinth with love.

<u>2 Corinthians 2:1-4</u>

> ¹ So I decided that I would not bring you grief with another painful visit. ² For if I cause you grief, who will make me glad? Certainly not someone I have grieved. ³ That is why I wrote to you as I did, so that when I do come, I won't be grieved by the very ones who ought to give me the greatest joy. Surely you all know that my joy comes from your being joyful. ⁴ I wrote that letter in great anguish, with a troubled heart and many tears. I didn't want to grieve you, but I wanted to let you know how much love I have for you.

<u>1 Thessalonians 3:5</u>

> ¹ Finally, when we could stand it no longer, we decided to stay alone in Athens, ² and we sent Timothy to visit you. He is our brother and God's co-worker in proclaiming the Good News of Christ. We sent him to strengthen you, to encourage you in your faith, ³ and to keep you from being

shaken by the troubles you were going through. But you know that we are destined for such troubles. ⁴Even while we were with you, we warned you that troubles would soon come—and they did, as you well know. ⁵That is why, when I could bear it no longer, I sent Timothy to find out whether your faith was still strong. I was afraid that the tempter had gotten the best of you and that our work had been useless.

Busyness

Even the amazing Moses was told that he was doing too much. His father-in-law cautioned him to start delegating, or else, he warned that "You're going to wear yourself out—and the people, too. This job is too heavy a burden for you to handle all by yourself" (Exodus 18:18). Even Jesus, who of all people certainly had a lot on His plate, never seemed to hurry. He says in John 17:4 that "I brought glory to you here on earth by completing the work you gave me to do." And yet, there were obviously people who were still not healed, not saved, not touched by His power. This is not a new thought, but it bears repeating. It's a lesson I am still learning. Jesus did *only* what God told Him to do. We all know that we take on too much, say "yes" too often, and mistake the need for the call. Trying to fill a hole because someone asked you is pointless, and it can cause strife and frustration. My part-time hobby is being an actress, on stage and on film. Because I don't know how to say "no" very well, I agreed to help backstage on a production. It involved many, many hours, and my husband and my current house guest suffered. Again, Jesus said it best: "I know where I came from and where I am going." (John 8:14, NIV). Figuring out the specific purpose that God designed you for is crucial.

We mistake being busy for being productive. But how did being productive come to be the highest goal? Charles Hummel says it best in his book *Freedom From Tyranny of the Urgent*.

> We live in constant tension between the urgent and the important. The problem is that many important tasks need not be done today, or even this week. Additional hours for prayer and Bible study, a visit to an elderly friend, reading an important book: these activities can usually wait a while longer. But often urgent, but less important, tasks call for immediate response and gobble up our time. . . We realize we have become slaves to the tyranny of the urgent.[28]

POINTS TO PONDER:

Read Matthew 11:28 again. "Are you tired? Worn out? Burned out on religion? Come to me. Get away with me and you'll recover your life."

Instead of "doing" something right now, take as long as your schedule allows to just sit with Jesus. This is a hard skill to learn, and we all need practice.

PRAYER:

Sovereign Lord, it is an effort for me to just pray. I confess that I don't feel like pursuing You right now. Thank You for Your presence and for allowing me to just sit here."

23
BURN OUT, PART 2

"Those who believe
they can do something
and those who believe they
can't are both right."

- HENRY FORD

Let's spend a little time looking at the warning signs that you are feeling burned out. Perhaps you read the previous chapter and thought, "this doesn't apply to me." I pray that is true, but let's examine some of the indicators so that you can recognize burnout or depression when/if they occur.

Depression

First of all, yes, even Christians get depressed.

> Psalm 143:7-8
>
> Come quickly, Lord, and answer me, for my depression deepens. Don't turn away from me, or I will die. Let me hear of your unfailing love each morning, for I am trusting you. Show me where to walk, for I give myself to you.
>
> Job 30:16
>
> And now my life seeps away. Depression haunts my days.

Signs include having little interest in doing things, little energy, trouble sleeping, trouble making decisions, a poor appetite, etc. If your depression is ongoing, you may want to visit a doctor. You could have a chemical imbalance or need counseling.

Apathy is a lighter form of depression. Pastor Dresselhaus used to say that if we saw someone raised from the dead every week at church we would soon get bored with it. Do you need constant stimulus? I think I am addicted to what is NEW. I love going to new restaurants, new parks, and new towns. Maybe this is because I moved constantly as a child. Growing up, I attended eight different schools before college.

Bitterness

A woman in the Old Testament was so frustrated with the way her life had turned out that she blamed God and even changed her name. "'Don't call me Naomi,' she responded. 'Instead, call me Mara, for the Almighty has made life very bitter for me'" (Ruth 1:20). Bitterness usually comes from not getting what we want, like Hannah suffering from infertility. "Hannah was in deep anguish, crying bitterly as she prayed to the Lord" (1 Samuel 1:10). I can relate to Hannah, who wanted a child so badly. As in her case, sometimes feeling bitter seems totally justified. Even those with great power are not immune.

2 Kings 20:1-3

About that time Hezekiah became deathly ill, and the prophet Isaiah son of Amoz went to visit him. He gave the king this message: "This is what the Lord says: Set your affairs in order, for you are going to die. You will not recover from this illness." ² When Hezekiah heard this, he turned his face to the wall and prayed to the Lord, ³ "Remember, O Lord, how I have always been faithful to you and have served you single-mindedly, always doing what pleases you." Then he broke down and wept bitterly.

Bitterness has a nasty way of spreading to others. It is contagious and ruins your witness.

James 3:10-12

¹⁰ And so blessing and cursing come pouring out of the same mouth. Surely, my brothers and sisters, this is not right! ¹¹ Does a spring of water bubble out with both fresh water and bitter water? ¹² Does a fig tree produce olives, or a grapevine produce figs? No, and you can't draw fresh water from a salty spring.

Hebrews 12:14-15

Work at living in peace with everyone, and work at living a holy life, for those who are not holy will not see the Lord. ¹⁵ Look after each other so that none of you fails to receive the grace of God. Watch out that no poisonous root of bitterness grows up to trouble you, corrupting many.

The good news is that God does listen to us. Even when we act like petulant children, He is paying attention. Read the next part of Hezekiah's story to see what I mean.

2 Kings 20:4-6

⁴ But before Isaiah had left the middle courtyard, this message came to him from the Lord: ⁵ "Go back to Hezekiah, the leader

of my people. Tell him, 'This is what the Lord, the God of your ancestor David, says: I have heard your prayer and seen your tears. I will heal you, and three days from now you will get out of bed and go to the Temple of the Lord.⁶ I will add fifteen years to your life, and I will rescue you and this city from the king of Assyria. I will defend this city for my own honor and for the sake of my servant David.'"

Whatever happens, don't let bitterness keep you from a relationship with God. One of the things I love most about the character of Job is his honesty. He lets his Father have it all, his anger and all the raw emotion inside him. "I cannot keep from speaking. I must express my anguish. My bitter soul must complain" (Job 7:11). "I am disgusted with my life. Let me complain freely. My bitter soul must complain" (Job 10:1).

After you are done venting, do what the psalmist below did: go into the presence of God and realize how "torn up inside" you are. Then, let the bitterness subside.

<u>Psalm 73:2-5, 13-14, 16-17, 21-25</u>

² But as for me, I almost lost my footing.
My feet were slipping, and I was almost gone.
³ For I envied the proud
when I saw them prosper despite their wickedness.
⁴ They seem to live such painless lives;
their bodies are so healthy and strong.
⁵ They don't have troubles like other people;
they're not plagued with problems like everyone else.
¹³ Did I keep my heart pure for nothing?
Did I keep myself innocent for no reason?
¹⁴ I get nothing but trouble all day long;
every morning brings me pain.
¹⁶ So I tried to understand why the wicked prosper.
But what a difficult task it is!
¹⁷ Then I went into your sanctuary, O God,
and I finally understood the destiny of the wicked.
²¹ Then I realized that my heart was bitter,
and I was all torn up inside.
²² I was so foolish and ignorant—

I must have seemed like a senseless animal to you.
²³ Yet I still belong to you;
you hold my right hand.
²⁴ You guide me with your counsel,
leading me to a glorious destiny.
²⁵ Whom have I in heaven but you?
I desire you more than anything on earth.

Avoiding Fellowship

D.L. Moody once spoke with a man who said he didn't need to go to church. In response, Moody reached into the fireplace and moved one coal away from the others. The two sat and watched the lone coal slowly die. In the passage below, we see that the battle would not have been won if Moses had refused the support of Aaron and Hur.

Exodus 17:8-13

While the people of Israel were still at Rephidim, the warriors of Amalek attacked them. ⁹ Moses commanded Joshua, "Choose some men to go out and fight the army of Amalek for us. Tomorrow, I will stand at the top of the hill, holding the staff of God in my hand." ¹⁰ So Joshua did what Moses had commanded and fought the army of Amalek. Meanwhile, Moses, Aaron, and Hur climbed to the top of a nearby hill. ¹¹ As long as Moses held up the staff in his hand, the Israelites had the advantage. But whenever he dropped his hand, the Amalekites gained the advantage. ¹² Moses' arms soon became so tired he could no longer hold them up. So Aaron and Hur found a stone for him to sit on. Then they stood on each side of Moses, holding up his hands. So his hands held steady until sunset. ¹³ As a result, Joshua overwhelmed the army of Amalek in battle.

Sisters: we need each other desperately! I am still finding out that friends I thought I knew well have deep hurt. This saddens me since we should be exposing the pain to each other and letting His sunlight shine upon it.

Think of ways you can reach out to others more often. Perhaps you can call someone who has missed church a few times or send a "Thinking of You" card or make a coffee date.

<u>Hebrews 10:24-25</u>

> Let us think of ways to motivate one another to acts of love and good works. [25] And let us not neglect our meeting together, as some people do, but encourage one another, especially now that the day of his return is drawing near.

There are many reasons why believers may stop going to church. Or, they may go on Sundays but be unwilling to involve themselves in small groups or other activities. Perhaps they have issues with the leadership or other saints in the pews. In this case, remember Philippians 2:14 "Do everything without complaining and arguing" and try to practice Hebrews 12:2, "fixing our eyes on Jesus" (NASB).

Perhaps someone has grown uncomfortable in worship, and so they choose to avoid that situation. They may have strained conversations with other Christians when talking about faith. Some may notice that they are not as apt to intercede for others as they used to be.

<u>1 Samuel 12:23 (NIV)</u>

> As for me, far be it from me that I should sin against the Lord by failing to pray for you

<u>Letting Discipline Slip</u>

There are days when it is a struggle to pick up the Bible, and there are days when I am not victorious. No one is perfect all the time, but we need to keep an eye on our habits. I know that even when I don't feel like praying, I need to bring the needs of those around me before the Lord because that is part of being the Body of Christ. As I'm writing this, I am very torn because I have a novel that I'm dying to finish. It's very difficult to work on my spiritual stuff first.

<u>Exodus 29:42</u> (Living Bible)

> This shall be a perpetual daily offering at the door of the Tabernacle before the Lord, where I will meet with you and speak with you.

POINTS TO PONDER:

Which of the subjects in this chapter has affected you most: depression, bitterness, avoiding fellowship, or letting discipline slip? Write down one step that you can take this week to work on this obstacle in your spiritual journey.

PRAYER:

Immanuel, God With Us, point out to my spirit any signs of burnout that I need to address. Help me to find refreshment in Your presence.

24
Voice of God

"Our lack of intimacy is due to our refusal to unplug and shut off communication from all others so we can be alone with Him."

- Francis Chan

Most of the time when believers talk about wanting to hear from the Lord they mean in an inner peace sort of way. Occasionally, though, He is almost audible. When I was a high school senior in northern California and still didn't know God personally, I went on a picnic with Christian friends on the top of Mount Diablo (ironically, Devil's Mountain). I was sitting apart from the group who was singing as usual. I was soaking in all the magnificent beauty of the hills and sky when something deep within me, not quite a voice but decidedly different than anything I'd felt in the past, said, "Who created these hills?" I whispered, "You did," and then got the feeling that He was asking me what I intended to do with that knowledge. I didn't have any choice left: I accepted Jesus as Lord without knowing the formula prayer to recite, just feeling very sure of His presence.

My brother has a similar story about meeting his wife for the first time. After a long night of talking and sharing, he got home, dropped to his knees, and asked God, "Is she the one?" He swears that he heard very plainly: "Yes."

I share these stories not because you should go around expecting God to speak up constantly, but because the reality is that He very much does want to communicate, and we shouldn't limit His methods.

Know His Word

Perhaps the most common way the Lord gets His point across is through His Word. I was discipling a young woman in Chicago. She had been attending a different church that insisted you had to be water baptized in order to be saved. She was really struggling with this, mostly because she didn't understand why her new church home didn't follow that theology. I tried every argument I could imagine and finally (thank you, Jesus) found some verses that made all the difference (1 Corinthians 1:13-17, if you're curious). She said "the light bulb turned on" and started dancing around the room in a joyous celebration that God had spoken to her.

Do you have a situation in your life right now that is confusing? Would you like to know God's opinion?

Accept Godly Advice

Why is talking to others important? It seems that, especially when it comes to romance, we turn our spiritual hearing aids off. When

I was much younger, my group of friends asked me to caution one of our sisters against marrying her fiancé. She got angry, of course, and got married anyway. Later, he abandoned her. You would think that would have taught me an important lesson, but fast forward a few years, and I was the one ignoring sage relationship advice.

Proverbs 11:14

Without wise leadership, a nation falls;
there is safety in having many advisers.

Proverbs 13:10

Pride leads to conflict; those who take advice are wise.

Proverbs 15:22

Plans go wrong for lack of advice; many advisers bring success.

How do the above Proverbs compare to traditional thinking that says "too many cooks spoil the broth"? How can you ensure that you are getting good advice?

Have Peace in Your Heart

Can you remember a time when God brought peace to your heart? What is the difference between peace and apathy, indifference and giving up?

Colossians 3:15

And let the peace that comes from Christ rule in your hearts. For as members of one body you are called to live in peace. And always be thankful.

Philippians 4:6-7

Don't worry about anything; instead, pray about everything. Tell God what you need and thank him for all he has done. [7] Then you will experience God's peace, which exceeds anything we can understand. His peace will guard your hearts and minds as you live in Christ Jesus.

John 14:27

"I am leaving you with a gift—peace of mind and heart. And the peace I give is a gift the world cannot give. So don't be troubled or afraid."

If you want to dig deeper, research Bible characters who felt peace during difficult trials, like Daniel in the lions' den or Paul before getting shipwrecked or Steven as he was being stoned.

The feeling of peace can be deceptive. What would you say to someone who says, "I don't feel guilty about _____. I have peace in my heart about it."?

Take Time to Wait on the Lord

What does waiting have to do with hearing the voice of God?

Psalm 27:14

Wait patiently for the Lord. Be brave and courageous. Yes, wait patiently for the Lord.

Isaiah 64:4

For since the world began, no ear has heard and no eye has seen a God like you, who works for those who wait for him!

Hebrews 6:15

Then Abraham waited patiently, and he received what God had promised.

Think of a circumstance in your life where waiting may have saved you from future trouble. What kinds of things might God teach you while you wait? (Patience? Faith? Determination?)

Listen Up!

The Holy Spirit uses those who pay attention. You probably have your own stories like the following one. My husband woke up in the middle of the night recently and felt that he should pray for a friend. Bob did not know it, but his friend Patrick was traveling. At the exact same time (4:00 a.m.), Patrick was driving, getting sleepy, and almost hit a deer.

POINTS TO PONDER:

<u>Deuteronomy 4:10-13</u> (The Message)

¹⁰That day when you stood before God, your God, at Horeb, God said to me, "Assemble the people in my presence to listen to my words so that they will learn to fear me in holy fear for as long as they live on the land, and then they will teach these same words to their children."

¹¹⁻¹³You gathered. You stood in the shadow of the mountain. The mountain was ablaze with fire, blazing high into the very heart of Heaven. You stood in deep darkness and thick clouds. God spoke to you out of the fire. You heard the sound of words but you saw nothing—no form, only a voice. He announced his covenant, the Ten Words, by which he commanded you to live. Then he wrote them down on two slabs of stone.

Close your eyes and try to visualize the scene. What do you feel as a voice comes out of the fire? What is your reaction when you read the Ten Commandments for the first time?

Do you truly want to hear the voice of our Lord? Are you excited to know what He has to say to you, or are you nervous?

PRAYER:

I come to You, the God Who Sees Me, in reverence. I want to hear You and obey, yet I am afraid of Your holiness. Give me the courage to pursue You and trust in Your unconditional love for me.

25

Hard-hearted

"I do not think much of a man
who is not wiser today than
he was yesterday."

- Abraham Lincoln

Most people do not deny their faith suddenly and commit a sin that would have been unthinkable to them one week prior. There are usually signs along the way, and we can either pay attention or choose to ignore them. I didn't gain 45 lbs. overnight after my wedding. Friends don't fall away from church after missing one Sunday. Alcoholics don't get addicted after one drink. We make choices every day.

When he met Bathsheba, David was not leading the army. He was not where God had designated him to be as a king. This is his prayer after his failures.

Psalm 51:1-6

[1] Have mercy on me, O God,
because of your unfailing love.
Because of your great compassion,
blot out the stain of my sins.
[2] Wash me clean from my guilt.
Purify me from my sin.
[3] For I recognize my rebellion;
it haunts me day and night.
[4] Against you, and you alone, have I sinned;
I have done what is evil in your sight.
You will be proved right in what you say,
and your judgment against me is just.
[5] For I was born a sinner—
yes, from the moment my mother conceived me.
[6] But you desire honesty from the womb,
teaching me wisdom even there.

What is David's attitude? Why is this important? What does he recognize about his sin? What do we tend to omit when praying about our own sin?

Psalm 51:7-11

[7] Purify me from my sins, and I will be clean;
wash me, and I will be whiter than snow.
[8] Oh, give me back my joy again;
you have broken me—

now let me rejoice.
⁹ Don't keep looking at my sins.
Remove the stain of my guilt.
¹⁰ Create in me a clean heart, O God.
Renew a loyal spirit within me.
¹¹ Do not banish me from your presence,
and don't take your Holy Spirit from me.

Why is David confident? What does he know he needs?

Psalm 51:13-17

¹³ Then I will teach your ways to rebels,
and they will return to you.
¹⁴ Forgive me for shedding blood, O God who saves;
then I will joyfully sing of your forgiveness.
¹⁵ Unseal my lips, O Lord,
that my mouth may praise you.
¹⁶ You do not desire a sacrifice, or I would offer one.
You do not want a burnt offering.
¹⁷ The sacrifice you desire is a broken spirit.
You will not reject a broken and repentant heart, O God.
¹⁸ Look with favor on Zion and help her;
rebuild the walls of Jerusalem.
¹⁹ Then you will be pleased with sacrifices offered in the right spirit—
with burnt offerings and whole burnt offerings.
Then bulls will again be sacrificed on your altar.

What happens in a believer's life after being forgiven? What does verse 17 mean to you? Some of my own struggles with sin came from dating men who were not strong believers. That first choice led to an inevitable battle about how far is too far because they were not as committed as I was to purity. Regular confession prevents entanglement in moral breakdown.

Genesis 4:7b

Sin is crouching at the door, eager to control you. But you must subdue it and be its master.

<u>James 1:14-15</u>

¹⁴Temptation comes from our own desires, which entice us and drag us away. ¹⁵These desires give birth to sinful actions. And when sin is allowed to grow, it gives birth to death.

<u>Psalm 66:16-20</u>

¹⁶Come and listen, all you who fear God,
and I will tell you what he did for me.
¹⁷For I cried out to him for help,
praising him as I spoke.
¹⁸If I had not confessed the sin in my heart,
the Lord would not have listened.
¹⁹But God did listen!
He paid attention to my prayer.
²⁰Praise God, who did not ignore my prayer
or withdraw his unfailing love from me.

<u>Psalm 32:5</u>

Finally, I confessed all my sins to you and stopped trying to hide my guilt. I said to myself, "I will confess my rebellion to the Lord." And you forgave me! All my guilt is gone.

How does sin prevent us from hearing God clearly? How easy is it to confess to God regularly?

> I begin with confession not in order to feel miserable, rather to call to mind a reality I often ignore. When I acknowledge where I stand before a perfect God, it restores the true state of the universe. Confession simply establishes the proper ground rules of creatures relating to their creator.[29]

> A human being is not someone who once in a while makes a mistake, and God is not someone who now and then forgives. No, human beings *are* sinners and God is love.[30]

Some people think confession is not necessary. They know that God is slow to anger, which is true and they mistakenly think that He is indulgent. I hope this is not your case and invite you to ponder the following.

Galatians 6:7-8 (The Message)

Don't be misled: No one makes a fool of God. What a person plants, he will harvest. The person who plants selfishness, ignoring the needs of others—ignoring God!—harvests a crop of weeds. All he'll have to show for his life is weeds! But the one who plants in response to God, letting God's Spirit do the growth work in him, harvests a crop of real life, eternal life.

John 14:15, 21

[14] If you love me, obey my commandments.... [21] Those who accept my commandments and obey them are the ones who love me. And because they love me, my Father will love them. And I will love them and reveal myself to each of them.

Hebrews 12:5-9

[5] And have you forgotten the encouraging words God spoke to you as his children? He said,
"My child, don't make light of the Lord's discipline,
and don't give up when he corrects you.
[6] For the Lord disciplines those he loves,
and he punishes each one he accepts as his child."
[7] As you endure this divine discipline, remember that God is treating you as his own children. Who ever heard of a child who is never disciplined by its father? [8] If God doesn't discipline you as he does all of his children, it means that you are illegitimate and are not really his children at all.
[9] Since we respected our earthly fathers who disciplined us, shouldn't we submit even more to the discipline of the Father of our spirits, and live forever?

Bob and I just attended a cowboy church because Bob dreams of starting one in Wisconsin. Pastor Joe Penrose told us to keep in mind that God's discipline is done in love, with the purpose of preparing you for a better future. It is not punishment for the past performed in anger.

We may also fall into the trap of thinking that our brand of sin isn't really all that bad. Considering the evil that exists in the world, is God really so concerned about my gluttony or gossiping or lust? Habakkuk 1:13a says, "Your eyes are too pure to look on evil; you cannot tolerate wrongdoing" (NASB).

A hardened heart may prevent us from hearing the voice of God.

Psalm 95:6-9

⁶Come, let us worship and bow down.
Let us kneel before the LORD our maker,
⁷for he is our God.
We are the people he watches over,
the flock under his care.
If only you would listen to his voice today!
⁸The Lord says, "Don't harden your hearts as Israel did at Meribah,
  as they did at Massah in the wilderness.
⁹ For there your ancestors tested and tried my patience,
even though they saw everything I did.

What does verse 8 have to do with verses 6 and 7? What might God be referring to in verse 9? What works of God have you seen? How does remembering these works help prevent you from having a hardened heart?

Exodus 17:1-7

¹At the Lord's command, the whole community of Israel left the wilderness of Sin and moved from place to place. Eventually they camped at Rephidim, but there was no water there for the people to drink. ² So once more the people complained against Moses. "Give us water to drink!" they demanded.

"Quiet!" Moses replied. "Why are you complaining against me? And why are you testing the Lord?"

³ But tormented by thirst, they continued to argue with Moses. "Why did you bring us out of Egypt? Are you trying to kill us, our children, and our livestock with thirst?"

⁴Then Moses cried out to the Lord, "What should I do with these people? They are ready to stone me!"

⁵The Lord said to Moses, "Walk out in front of the people. Take your staff, the one you used when you struck the water of the Nile, and call some of the elders of Israel to join you.

⁶I will stand before you on the rock at Mount Sinai. Strike the rock, and water will come gushing out. Then the people will be able to drink." So Moses struck the rock as he was told, and water gushed out as the elders looked on.

⁷Moses named the place Massah (which means "test") and Meribah (which means "arguing") because the people of Israel argued with Moses and tested the Lord by saying, "Is the Lord here with us or not?"

This story takes place after the Israelites have just been delivered from the hands of their Egyptian masters, as new believers are first set free from slavery to sin. Why are people grumbling? How do they show their lack of faith? What attitudes cause you to lose your focus when things get rough? How can you resist your heart hardening next time?

<u>Hebrews 3:12-15</u>

¹²Be careful then, dear brothers and sisters. Make sure that your own hearts are not evil and unbelieving, turning you away from the living God. ¹³You must warn each other every day, while it is still "today," so that none of you will be deceived by sin and hardened against God. ¹⁴For if we are faithful to the end, trusting God just as firmly as when we first believed, we will share in all that belongs to Christ. ¹⁵Remember what it says:

> "Today when you hear his voice,
> don't harden your hearts
> as Israel did when they rebelled."

What method is mentioned here to avoid having a hard heart? Think of three ways you can put this into practice.

<u>Hebrews 4:11-12</u>

⁹So there is a special rest still waiting for the people of God.
¹⁰For all who have entered into God's rest have rested from

their labors, just as God did after creating the world.[11] So let us do our best to enter that rest. But if we disobey God, as the people of Israel did, we will fall.

[12] For the word of God is alive and powerful. It is sharper than the sharpest two-edged sword, cutting between soul and spirit, between joint and marrow. It exposes our innermost thoughts and desires.

1. _____

2. _____

3. _____

How does God's word help keep your heart soft? Next time you are moved by His word, whether through your own reading or during a sermon, I challenge you to make an effort to remember this moment. Write it down during church, journal at home, or share with a friend.

Even as I write this, I know that I still struggle. I think of 2 Timothy 4:10 *(Demas has deserted me because he loves the things of this life)*. I have never deserted God completely, yet multiple times a given day, I choose my desires and ignore His voice. If your daily discipline is slipping, do a self-examination of your heart. I have a church friend who can't fall asleep at night if she hasn't read at least one verse of the Bible. Make sure that you are not using your freedom in Christ as an excuse to not pursue a relationship with your Maker. I am pretty sure my husband would not appreciate it if I went a day or more without talking to him!

Another small sign of moral breakdown is plain old discontentment. It can creep up very subtly. Don't covet your neighbor's wife really means stop comparing yourself to others. And sisters, you know how prone we are to this habit. It takes practice, but try to be happy for your friend who is more slender or who got a better job or who is dating that cute guy. Don't give the devil a foothold to worm his nastiness into your soul.

POINTS TO PONDER:

Verse 12 of Psalm 51 says "Restore to me the joy of your salvation and make me willing to obey you." Paraphrase this for yourself. Why do you think David asks for joy?

PRAYER:

Heavenly Father, I tremble when I think of how hard-hearted I can be at times. Give me the willingness to repent quickly and help me want to please You more.

26
Perfect Woman

"If you want God to bless you and use you greatly, you must be willing to walk with a limp the rest of your life, because God uses weak people."

- Rick Warren

Decades ago, a woman in my church prophesied over me. She said, "You have not let God down." It hit me really hard because that was how I had felt my whole life. Unfortunately, I think this is a common theme.

Close your eyes and picture the perfect Christian woman. What is she wearing? What is she talking about? How pretty/thin/tall is she? If you are like me, an image immediately comes to mind. For me, the idea of the woman I should strive to become came from my senior pastor's wife. She was elegant, refined, gentle, wise, and caring. In every way, I felt like the complete opposite.

Years later, serving as a missionary just made things worse. I felt like an imposter. I had the mom of five kids tell me how jealous she was of my life because as a single woman, I must get to pray all the time! I felt so ashamed that she probably had a more intimate walk with Jesus than I did at the time.

Reading verses like the ones below did not help!

1 Peter 3:3-5

[3] Do not let your beauty come from the outside. It should not be the way you comb your hair or the wearing of gold or the wearing of fine clothes. [4] Your beauty should come from the inside. It should come from the heart. This is the kind that lasts. Your beauty should be a gentle and quiet spirit. In God's sight this is of great worth and no amount of money can buy it. [5] This was the kind of beauty seen in the holy women who lived many years ago. They put their hope in God. They also obeyed their husbands.

1 Timothy 2:11-13

[11] Women should be quiet when they learn. They should listen to what men have to say. [12] I never let women teach men or be leaders over men. They should be quiet. [13] Adam was made first, then Eve.

Titus 2:3

[3] Teach older women to be quiet and to be careful how they act also. They are not to go around speaking bad things about others or things that are not true. They are not to be chained by strong drink. They should teach what is good.

What stands out to you from these verses?

For me, the word "quiet" screamed out. I am anything but quiet. I always want to have the last word. I am an on-again-off-again professional actor, and I have no problem speaking my mind in front of people. So how do I take this loud-mouthed, sometimes bossy, opinionated person and make her meek and mild?

First, I had to not only accept who I was but LOVE myself. What? Have you ever tried to apply the love chapter to yourself?

1 Corinthians 13:4-7

⁴ Love is patient and kind. Love is not jealous or boastful or proud ⁵ or rude. It does not demand its own way. It is not irritable, and it keeps no record of being wronged. ⁶ It does not rejoice about injustice but rejoices whenever the truth wins out. ⁷ Love never gives up, never loses faith, is always hopeful, and endures through every circumstance.

"Love is patient." When you promise to read a chapter in the Bible every day and you skip two days in a row, are you patient with yourself? How would you treat a friend who told you she did that?

"Love is not jealous." Can you learn to take appropriate pride in your own accomplishments without placing negative focus on someone else's gifts?

Galatians 6:4-5 (The Message)

Make a careful exploration of who you are and the work you have been given, and then sink yourself into that. Don't be impressed with yourself. Don't compare yourself with others. Each of you must take responsibility for doing the creative best you can with your own life.

Love is not "boastful or proud." Are you confident enough to shine for Jesus without pointing it out?

Romans 12:16 (Amplified Bible)

Live in harmony with one another; do not be haughty (snobbish, high-minded, exclusive), but readily adjust yourself to [people, things] *and* give yourselves to humble tasks. Never overestimate yourself *or* be wise in your own conceits.

Love "keeps no record of being wronged. It does not rejoice about injustice." Read how the Lord treats you.

Psalm 103:8-14

⁸ The Lord is compassionate and merciful,
slow to get angry and filled with unfailing love.
⁹ He will not constantly accuse us,
nor remain angry forever.
¹⁰ He does not punish us for all our sins;
he does not deal harshly with us, as we deserve.
¹¹ For his unfailing love toward those who fear him
is as great as the height of the heavens above the earth.
¹² He has removed our sins as far from us
as the east is from the west.
¹³ The Lord is like a father to his children,
tender and compassionate to those who fear him.
¹⁴ For he knows how weak we are;
he remembers we are only dust.

If God is willing to treat you so compassionately, shouldn't you do the same for yourself? Confess, then forgive yourself. Learn from your mistakes rather than lingering on them. Sometimes guilt takes the place of true repentance, and we wallow in it.

"Love never gives up, never loses faith, is always hopeful, and endures through every circumstance." Do you have faith in yourself? Can you say, "I can do everything through Christ, who gives me strength" (Philippians 4:13)? Are you hopeful about yourself, striving to become the best you can be for God? Do you have staying power—determination in spite of failure or difficult circumstances?

I had to learn to rejoice in who I am and not covet someone else's strengths. But I also needed to avoid getting a big head about my own giftedness. To paraphrase C.S. Lewis, you can no more be proud of your talents than you can boast about having blue eyes.

Everything about you is given by God. Use what you have for His kingdom's work and stop comparing yourself to others.

Ecclesiastes 7:21

[21] Do not pay attention to every word people say,
or you may hear your servant cursing you—
[22] for you know in your heart
that many times you yourself have cursed others.

1 Corinthians 4:6-7

[6] Christian brothers, I have used Apollos and myself to show you what I am talking about. This is to help you so you will not think more of men than what God's Word will allow. Never think more of one of God's servants than another. [7] Who made you better than your brother? Or what do you have that has not been given to you? If God has given you everything, why do you have pride? Why do you act as if He did not give it to you?

Sisters, we are especially prone to looking to others for approval. There was one time that I received some interesting feedback on my apparel. Many years ago, our four-year-old grandson was spending the weekend with us. I came out of the bedroom wearing a long, gold, fringed dress feeling fairly attractive. He put his hands on his little hips, looked me square in the eyes, and firmly stated, "No one is wearing *that* to church." I was flabbergasted and, of course, had to ask why? He whispered back: "They're going to call the police."

Beware of depending on others for approval! As with most things, balance is key. "Don't be impressed with yourself" from the above Galatians passage puts it very plainly. But you also don't want to make Mephibosheth's mistake.

2 Samuel 9:1-13

[3] The king then asked him, "Is anyone still alive from Saul's family? If so, I want to show God's kindness to them."

Ziba replied, "Yes, one of Jonathan's sons is still alive. He is crippled in both feet."

⁴ "Where is he?" the king asked.

"In Lo-debar," Ziba told him, "at the home of Makir son of Ammiel."

⁵ So David sent for him and brought him from Makir's home. ⁶ His name was Mephibosheth; he was Jonathan's son and Saul's grandson. When he came to David, he bowed low to the ground in deep respect. David said, "Greetings, Mephibosheth."

Mephibosheth replied, "I am your servant."

⁷ "Don't be afraid!" David said. "I intend to show kindness to you because of my promise to your father, Jonathan. I will give you all the property that once belonged to your grandfather Saul, and you will eat here with me at the king's table!"

⁸ Mephibosheth bowed respectfully and exclaimed, "Who is your servant, that you should show such kindness to a dead dog like me?"

How do you feel about who you are when you are alone? Can you visualize the woman that God delights in or do you see "a dead dog"? I once saw a cartoon of a man looking into a mirror and asking, "Well, are you for me or against me today?" A woman told me that her mother had a Bible that was inscribed: "From someone who loves you very much" which she had bought for herself! Did you know it takes four compliments to nullify one insult? It is okay to be good to yourself. Jesus was a great example of positive thinking. "I *will* draw all men unto Myself," "I *will* come again," "I *will* build My church."

Judy Rachels, a retreat speaker, explained that even Peter (the Rock) turned *away* from the Creator of the Universe to compare himself to someone else.

John 21:20-21

Peter turned around and saw behind them the disciple Jesus loved—the one who had leaned over to Jesus during supper and asked, "Lord, who will betray you?" [21] Peter asked Jesus, "What about him, Lord?"

We all fall short of the glory of God, but we only need to worry about how we measure up to Jesus—not each other. The best part is that grace makes up for everything that we lack.

God made each of us as an individual. If you let Him, He will use your personality for His glory.

Romans 9:20-21

[20] No, don't say that. Who are you, a mere human being, to argue with God? Should the thing that was created say to the one who created it, "Why have you made me like this?" [21] When a potter makes jars out of clay, doesn't he have a right to use the same lump of clay to make one jar for decoration and another to throw garbage into?

Isaiah 45:9

"What sorrow awaits those who argue with their Creator.
Does a clay pot argue with its maker?
Does the clay dispute with the one who shapes it, saying,
'Stop, you're doing it wrong!'
Does the pot exclaim,
'How clumsy can you be?'

Ephesians 2:10

For we are God's masterpiece. He has created us anew in Christ Jesus, so we can do the good things he planned for us long ago.

I saw a visual presentation by a speaker named Zoanne Wilkie. She referenced this passage:

2 Corinthians 4:6-7

[6] For God, who said, "Let there be light in the darkness," has made this light shine in our hearts so we could know the glory of God that is seen in the face of Jesus Christ.

[7] We now have this light shining in our hearts, but we ourselves are like fragile clay jars containing this great treasure. This

makes it clear that our great power is from God, not from ourselves.

Wilkie had a collection of cups that she was examining one by one. Some were real china, fragile and decorative. Others were oversized with big handles and sarcastic, humorous sayings. Others were completely utilitarian like red solo cups. The speaker picked up each cup and, pretending it was a person, told its story. The china cup was very proud of her gold feet and tiny delicate flowers. One large mug with a picture of a moose on it said, "God could never use me. I'll stay in the back and just pray." The Styrofoam cup was thinking, "I'm just trash." It was a great way to illustrate different personalities.

The clincher, though, was when Wilkie poured water into each of the cups. No matter the vessel holding it, Living Water tastes the same. It is what is inside of us that counts, not the packaging.

What keeps us from becoming who we are meant to be? For some, perhaps past hurt prevents them from living life to the fullest NOW.

Isaiah 43:18-19 (NIV)

[18] "Forget the former things;
do not dwell on the past.
[19] See, I am doing a new thing!
Now it springs up; do you not perceive it?

Ecclesiastes 5:19-20

[19] And it is a good thing to receive wealth from God and the good health to enjoy it. To enjoy your work and accept your lot in life—this is indeed a gift from God. [20] God keeps such people so busy enjoying life that they take no time to brood over the past.

Lamentations 3:19-20
[19] The thought of my suffering and homelessness
is bitter beyond words.
[20] I will never forget this awful time,
as I grieve over my loss.

Thankfully, Jeremiah, the author of Lamentations, did not dwell on his problems for too long. In the very next verse, he proclaims: "Yet

I still dare to hope when I remember this: The faithful love of the Lord never ends! His mercies never cease. Great is his faithfulness; his mercies begin afresh each morning (Lamentations 3:21-23).

Other believers may be stuck in a rut, too comfortable to spread their wings and see how God may want to use them.

Jeremiah 48:11

"From his earliest history, Moab has lived in peace,
never going into exile.
He is like wine that has been allowed to settle.
He has not been poured from flask to flask,
and he is now fragrant and smooth."

Moab had taken their land from a race of giants (Deuteronomy 2: 9-10) and was able to retain it and prosper without suffering. However, the spiritual consequence of comfortable living was never learning to have faith in God. Being "poured from flask to flask" improves the quality of the wine, separating the liquid from the dregs. Imagine yourself as wine. If we allow for complacency, we won't taste very good.

I believe that the majority of Christians do not have a vision for their future. How would it change your life to truly believe that "No eye has seen, no ear has heard, no mind has conceived what God has prepared for those who love Him" (1 Corinthians 2:9-10). Lift up your eyes!

Genesis 13:14-17 (NASB)

[14] The Lord said to Abram, after Lot had separated from him, "Now lift up your eyes and look from the place where you are, northward and southward and eastward and westward; [15] for all the land which you see, I will give it to you and to your descendants forever. [16] I will make your descendants as the dust of the earth, so that if anyone can number the dust of the earth, your descendants can also be numbered. [17] Arise, walk about the land through its length and breadth; for I will give it to you."

So to conclude, reaching the goal stated in Matthew 5:48 ("But you are to be perfect, even as your Father in heaven is perfect") is not unattainable at all.

POINTS TO PONDER:

If you were a cup, what would you look like? Can you visualize being filled with Living Water? Would this Living Water taste better if you looked different?

PRAYER:

El Elyon, Most High God, show me a glimpse of the woman You see when You look at me. Give me the confidence to be all I can be for Your glory.

27
Enlarged Territory

"A person who never made a mistake never tried anything new."

- Albert Einstein

This story involves moving out of your comfort zone: the first step to enlarging your territory.

> Joshua 3:1-5
>
> Early the next morning Joshua and all the Israelites left Acacia Grove and arrived at the banks of the Jordan River, where they camped before crossing. ²Three days later the Israelite officers went through the camp,³ giving these instructions to the people: "When you see the Levitical priests carrying the Ark of the Covenant of the Lord your God, move out from your positions and follow them. ⁴ Since you have never traveled this way before, they will guide you. Stay about half a mile behind them, keeping a clear distance between you and the Ark. Make sure you don't come any closer."
>
> ⁵Then Joshua told the people, "Purify yourselves, for tomorrow the Lord will do great wonders among you."

Look for the Ark Moving

What does the ark represent? Think about a time in your life when you knew God was up to something—either within your own spirit or outwardly through your circumstances.

Move Out from Your Position

When God begins to move in your life, it may involve leaving your comfort zone. Note that the NASB and NKJ versions don't say follow the ark, but "go after it." Don't you love the urgency? What would this look like in your life?

During my time as a missionary, I was asked to write the church's annual Easter play. At that time, I had very limited theater experience. I was completely out of my comfort zone, but God gave me the grace to not only write but also direct a performance where lives were changed for eternity.

Look for God's Guidance

God knows that "you have never traveled this way before," and He promises that "your own ears will hear him. Right behind you a voice will say, 'This is the way you should go,' whether to the right or to the left" (Isaiah 30:21). A year from now, you may be doing something entirely different in your ministry, in your relationships, in your personal time with God. How have you heard from God in the past? Do you think He will use the same method each time?

Stay Behind the Ark

What does this mean to you? What could the danger be in getting too close or too far ahead?

Purify Yourself

We no longer have elaborate cleansing rituals. What does this verse mean for a modern Christian? What do you need to cleanse before the Lord can work His power in you?

1 Chronicles 4:9-10

> There was a man named Jabez who was more honorable than any of his brothers. His mother named him Jabez because his birth had been so painful. [10] He was the one who prayed to the God of Israel, "Oh, that you would bless me and expand my territory! Please be with me in all that I do, and keep me from all trouble and pain!" And God granted him his request.

Bruce Wilkinson wrote the bestseller *The Prayer of Jabez*[31] based on the above verses. Wilkinson suggests that this unknown figure in the Bible wanted "more influence, more responsibility, and more opportunity to make a mark for the God of Israel." I'm sure that most of us would love for our lives to count for something, to have a significant purpose beyond going to work, taking care of family, watching TV, etc. But as Wilkinson states, most of us get stuck on the math when imagining what God might have in store for us. We think:

> "My abilities + experience + training + my personality and appearance + my past and the expectation of others = my assigned territory"

But God's math looks more like this:

> "My willingness and weakness + God's will and supernatural power = my expanding territory"

Verse 5 assures us that "the Lord will do great wonders." I can assure you that a mere 15 years ago it would NEVER have even occurred to me that I would now be: 1) a film actress; 2) Nana to 10 children; 3) married to a Nashville recording artist. My itsy-bitsy territory exploded beyond my wildest imagination. I cannot take any credit. God took my meager offerings like those of the boy with the loaves and fishes and presto! He did HIS thing.

Let's examine some principles about territories and how to expand our own.

<u>Psalm 119:30-32</u> (NASB)

> I have chosen the faithful way; I have placed Your ordinances before me. [31] I cling to Your testimonies; O Lord, do not put me to shame! [32] I shall run the way of Your commandments, For You will enlarge my heart.

If you are reading this and thinking, "Yes! I can't wait to do something big and important for God," then slow down. The first step to expanding your territory is clinging to His ways.

Principle #1: Pray for an enlarged heart before expanding territory

When the Jews fled Egypt, they were not grounded in a secure knowledge of God. After all, they had been living in the enemy's camp for hundreds of years. Yahweh knew they were not prepared for battle and therefore allowed them to meander. Let's not be like our ancestors who had to be rerouted.

<u>Exodus 13:17-18a</u>

> [17] When Pharaoh finally let the people go, God did not lead them along the main road that runs through Philistine territory, even though that was the shortest route to the Promised Land. God said, "If the people are faced with a battle, they might change their minds and return to Egypt." [18] So God led them in a roundabout way through the wilderness toward the Red Sea.

Principle #2: When you pray for your territory to enlarge, be prepared for spiritual warfare

Remember: It's not all about me.

Judges 1:3

The men of Judah said to their relatives from the tribe of Simeon, "Join with us to fight against the Canaanites living in the territory allotted to us. Then we will help you conquer your territory." So the men of Simeon went with Judah.

What can we do that enables our brothers and sisters to enlarge their territory? Does someone need encouragement? Discipling? Ask your friends this question: "If you had all the faith in the world that you wouldn't fail, what would you like to do for God's kingdom?" Then, start praying that the Lord will begin developing these dreams.

Joshua 1:10-15

[10] Joshua then commanded the officers of Israel, [11] "Go through the camp and tell the people to get their provisions ready. In three days you will cross the Jordan River and take possession of the land the Lord your God is giving you."

[12] Then Joshua called together the tribes of Reuben, Gad, and the half-tribe of Manasseh. He told them, [13] "Remember what Moses, the servant of the Lord, commanded you: 'The Lord your God is giving you a place of rest. He has given you this land.' [14] Your wives, children, and livestock may remain here in the land Moses assigned to you on the east side of the Jordan River. But your strong warriors, fully armed, must lead the other tribes across the Jordan to help them conquer their territory. Stay with them [15] until the Lord gives them rest, as he has given you rest, and until they, too, possess the land the Lord your God is giving them. Only then may you return and settle here on the east side of the Jordan River in the land that Moses, the servant of the Lord, assigned to you."

Our friend Joe had no vision of what to do with his music. He just knew that God had given him lyrics and he wrote them down. With the help of a team of friends, in his 60s, he went from playing at a few coffee houses to producing two CDs and a slew of videos. He had multiple songs on the charts, and his music played on the radio across Europe. Because of the support of others, his words have encouraged tens of thousands of people.

Principle #3: Encourage others to also expand their territories

Every time Joe was tempted to boast or strut, he felt the discipline of the Lord's hand. This was God's work, and Joe was meant to be the servant.

Exodus 34:24

I will drive out the other nations ahead of you and expand your territory, so no one will covet and conquer your land while you appear before the Lord your God.

2 Corinthians 10:15-17 (NASB)

[15] Nor do we boast and claim credit for the work someone else has done. Instead, we hope that your faith will grow so that the boundaries of our work among you will be extended. [16] Then we will be able to go and preach the Good News in other places far beyond you, where no one else is working. Then there will be no question of our boasting about work done in someone else's territory. [17] As the Scriptures say, "If you want to boast, boast only about the Lord."

Principle #4: The Lord is the one who will expand your territory

The process of gaining territory will be difficult, but we can respond in faith.

Psalm 31:7-8 (NASB)

I will be glad and rejoice in your love, for you saw my affliction and knew the anguish of my soul. [8] You have not given me into the hands of the enemy but have set my feet in a spacious place.

Principle #5: Continue to rejoice

Who have you already touched with the good news? Begin with your family and friends, and pray that opportunities will expand outward to those who have not heard the gospel. Maybe start a neighborhood coffee and chat time or babysit the kids of single moms.

Isaiah 54:1-6

Shout for joy, O barren one, you who have borne no *child;*
Break forth into joyful shouting and cry aloud, you who have

not travailed; For the sons of the desolate one *will be* more numerous than the sons of the married woman," says the Lord.

² "Enlarge the place of your tent; stretch out the curtains of your dwellings, spare not; lengthen your cords and strengthen your pegs. ³ "For you will spread abroad to the right and to the left. And your descendants will possess nations and will resettle the desolate cities. ⁴ "Fear not, for you will not be put to shame; and do not feel humiliated, for you will not be disgraced; but you will forget the shame of your youth, and the reproach of your widowhood you will remember no more. ⁵ "For your husband is your Maker, whose name is the Lord of hosts; and your Redeemer is the Holy One of Israel, who is called the God of all the earth. ⁶ "For the Lord has called you, like a wife forsaken and grieved in spirit, even like a wife of one's youth when she is rejected," says your God.

In my journal, I wrote the following.

We are not meant to live in a narrow, confined place surrounded by fears and enemies and worries and pain. We can live life in a spacious place where there is freedom to love and experience God's goodness. Part of obtaining that life is our choice—we are told to stretch the curtains of our tent back, lengthening the cords and not holding back. As we ourselves enlarge, the results for the kingdom will be great. Even me, who may be seen to have a narrow life without a husband and with little influence considering I have no children of my own, can expect more children (converts? disciples? those I have touched with truth and love?) than a married woman.

Isaiah 49:19-22

¹⁹ Even the most desolate parts of your abandoned land
will soon be crowded with your people.
Your enemies who enslaved you
will be far away.
²⁰ The generations born in exile will return and say,
'We need more room! It's crowded here!'

²¹ Then you will think to yourself,
'Who has given me all these descendants?
For most of my children were killed,
and the rest were carried away into exile.
I was left here all alone.
Where did all these people come from?
Who bore these children?
Who raised them for me?'"
²² This is what the Sovereign Lord says:
"See, I will give a signal to the godless nations.
They will carry your little sons back to you in their arms;
they will bring your daughters on their shoulders.

Principle #6: Begin at home and push out

What habits or thoughts or relationships need to be cleared out from your life so that you can enter and occupy the land?

Deuteronomy 7:16-24

¹⁶ "You must destroy all the nations the Lord your God hands over to you. Show them no mercy, and do not worship their gods, or they will trap you. ¹⁷ Perhaps you will think to yourselves, 'How can we ever conquer these nations that are so much more powerful than we are?' ¹⁸ But don't be afraid of them! Just remember what the Lord your God did to Pharaoh and to all the land of Egypt. ¹⁹ Remember the great terrors the Lord your God sent against them. You saw it all with your own eyes! And remember the miraculous signs and wonders, and the strong hand and powerful arm with which he brought you out of Egypt. The Lord your God will use this same power against all the people you fear. ²⁰ And then the Lord your God will send terror to drive out the few survivors still hiding from you!

²¹ "No, do not be afraid of those nations, for the Lord your God is among you, and he is a great and awesome God. ²² The Lord your God will drive those nations out ahead of you little by little. You will not clear them away all at once, otherwise the wild animals would multiply too quickly for you. ²³ But the Lord your God will hand them over to you. He will throw them into complete confusion until they are

destroyed. ²⁴ He will put their kings in your power, and you will erase their names from the face of the earth. No one will be able to stand against you, and you will destroy them all.

What is the spiritual principle from verse 22? Is there something you need to see accomplished in your life that seems to be taking too long? What purpose might the Lord have in helping you "little by little"?

POINTS TO PONDER:

Which principle of enlargement stood out to you most? Look up related verses and read them in their greater context.

PRAYER:

You are Jehovah Uzzi, The Lord My Strength. I ask for Your strength now to help me escape the confines of my day to day life and live boldly for You.

28
ENEMIES OF OUR MIND

"Satan puts straws across our path and magnifies it and makes us believe it is a mountain, but all the devil's mountains are mountains of smoke; when you come up to them they are not there."

- DWIGHT L. MOODY

Have you learned to recognize when the arch enemy of your soul is pestering you? Here is a passage from my journal on the topic.

> If Satan told me outright "God doesn't love you" I would recognize the lie and stand firm against it. Instead, he sends "little nagging thoughts, suspicions, doubts, fears"[32] to make me feel unimportant or overlooked. "He knows our insecurities, our weaknesses and our fears."[33] Lately, being single has been bothering me more. When I get self-obsessed, I complain, and I eat more and burrow into a deeper hole of self-pity. The devil is patient. He is willing to wait for me to lose my faith. I have to recognize these symptoms early on and fight. My mind is a battlefield, and I have an enemy. I need to use the weapons of prayer and praise.

It blows my mind how faithful God is. Rereading my journals as I write this book has given me such amazing gratitude for what He has done in my life. I have tremendous faith that He can do the same for you. I wrote the following passage just one week after the one above.

> "For as he thinks in his heart so is he" (Psalm 23:7). People would probably be surprised by the extent of my negative thinking—I even shock myself realizing how pessimistic I can be. I'll never get married, get out of debt, have a child, have sex, be successful, be a truly spiritual Christian, lose weight, have a satisfying career, afford to travel, own a home, etc. This kind of thinking crushes ambition and stops dreams before they even begin growing.

Hallelujah! Most of what I was sure would never come to pass has been granted to me by our Savior. Don't give up! One month later, I had begun to see some hope as I continued reading *Battlefield of the Mind* by Joyce Meyer.

> I need to have purpose in my prayer and praise/worship. Spending time with God is a VITAL NECESSITY, not an option. I need to stop thinking that I am not going anywhere. I need to stop thinking that I am unmotivated, lazy, or doomed to be an old maid person. If I don't believe in myself, who will?

I need to walk in the knowledge of "being more than a conqueror" and anticipate a future of hope.

The first step in fighting the enemies in our mind is identifying them. By enemies I mean those things that wage war against our soul: depression, loneliness, fear, insecurity, anger, bitterness. Which has been threatening you recently?

Read the following passage. How does this Psalm help explain your feelings when being attacked?

Psalm 143:3-12

3 My enemy has chased me.
He has knocked me to the ground
and forces me to live in darkness like those in the grave.
4 I am losing all hope;
I am paralyzed with fear.
5 I remember the days of old.
I ponder all your great works
and think about what you have done.
6 I lift my hands to you in prayer.
I thirst for you as parched land thirsts for rain. *Interlude*
7 Come quickly, Lord, and answer me,
for my depression deepens.
Don't turn away from me,
or I will die.
8 Let me hear of your unfailing love each morning,
for I am trusting you.
Show me where to walk,
for I give myself to you.
9 Rescue me from my enemies, LORD;
I run to you to hide me.
10 Teach me to do your will,
for you are my God.
May your gracious Spirit lead me forward
on a firm footing.
11 For the glory of your name, O Lord, preserve my life.
Because of your faithfulness, bring me out of this distress.
12 In your unfailing love, silence all my enemies
and destroy all my foes,
for I am your servant.

Choose one verse from this passage that you would like to memorize.

As you read the verses below, highlight all the ways that God responds when we are facing an enemy.

Deuteronomy 33:26-27

[26] "There is no one like the God of Israel.
He rides across the heavens to help you,
across the skies in majestic splendor.
[27] The eternal God is your refuge,
and his everlasting arms are under you.
He drives out the enemy before you;
he cries out, 'Destroy them!'

2 Samuel 22:30-38

[30] In your strength I can crush an army;
with my God I can scale any wall.
[31] "God's way is perfect.
All the Lord's promises prove true.
He is a shield for all who look to him for protection.
[32] For who is God except the Lord?
Who but our God is a solid rock?
[33] God is my strong fortress,
and he makes my way perfect.
[34] He makes me as surefooted as a deer,
enabling me to stand on mountain heights.
[35] He trains my hands for battle;
he strengthens my arm to draw a bronze bow.
[36] You have given me your shield of victory;
your help has made me great.
[37] You have made a wide path for my feet
to keep them from slipping.
[38] "I chased my enemies and destroyed them;
I did not stop until they were conquered.

Psalm 31:8

You have not handed me over to my enemies
but have set me in a safe place.

Psalm 41:11-12

[11] I know you are pleased with me,

for you have not let my enemies triumph over me.
¹² You have preserved my life because I am innocent;
you have brought me into your presence forever.

Joshua 23:10

Each one of you will put to flight a thousand of the enemy,
for the Lord your God fights for you, just as he has promised.

Isaiah 33:2-3a

² But Lord, be merciful to us,
for we have waited for you.
Be our strong arm each day
and our salvation in times of trouble.
³ The enemy runs at the sound of your voice.

It can feel like we are the only one in the universe who hurts. Underline the phrases from the following verses that describe how you feel (or have felt). Circle the passages with good news.

Psalm 13:1-6

¹ O Lord, how long will you forget me? Forever?
How long will you look the other way?
² How long must I struggle with anguish in my soul,
with sorrow in my heart every day?
How long will my enemy have the upper hand?
³ Turn and answer me, O Lord my God!
Restore the sparkle to my eyes, or I will die.
⁴ Don't let my enemies gloat, saying, "We have defeated him!"
Don't let them rejoice at my downfall.
⁵ But I trust in your unfailing love.
I will rejoice because you have rescued me.
⁶ I will sing to the Lord
because he is good to me.

Psalm 61:1-3

O God, listen to my cry!
Hear my prayer!
² From the ends of the earth,
I cry to you for help

when my heart is overwhelmed.
Lead me to the towering rock of safety,
³ for you are my safe refuge,
a fortress where my enemies cannot reach me.

Psalm 62:3-7

³ So many enemies against one man—
all of them trying to kill me.
To them I'm just a broken-down wall
or a tottering fence.
⁴ They plan to topple me from my high position.
They delight in telling lies about me.
They praise me to my face
but curse me in their hearts. *Interlude*

⁵ Let all that I am wait quietly before God,
for my hope is in him.
⁶ He alone is my rock and my salvation,
my fortress where I will not be shaken.
⁷ My victory and honor come from God alone.
He is my refuge, a rock where no enemy can reach me.

Micah 7:5-8

⁵ Don't trust anyone—
not your best friend or even your wife!
⁶ For the son despises his father.
The daughter defies her mother.
The daughter-in-law defies her mother-in-law.
Your enemies are right in your own household!

⁷ As for me, I look to the Lord for help.
I wait confidently for God to save me,
and my God will certainly hear me.
⁸ Do not gloat over me, my enemies!
For though I fall, I will rise again.
Though I sit in darkness,
the Lord will be my light.

Luke 10:19-20

¹⁹ Look, I have given you authority over all the power of the enemy, and you can walk among snakes and scorpions

and crush them. Nothing will injure you. [20] But don't rejoice because evil spirits obey you; rejoice because your names are registered in heaven."

Ephesians 6:10-13

[10] A final word: Be strong in the Lord and in his mighty power. [11] Put on all of God's armor so that you will be able to stand firm against all strategies of the devil. [12] For we are not fighting against flesh-and-blood enemies, but against evil rulers and authorities of the unseen world, against mighty powers in this dark world, and against evil spirits in the heavenly places.

[13] Therefore, put on every piece of God's armor so you will be able to resist the enemy in the time of evil. Then after the battle you will still be standing firm.

For me, the time of greatest spiritual warfare occurred during my first year in Chicago. I knew 1 Peter 5:8 ("Stay alert! Watch out for your great enemy, the devil. He prowls around like a roaring lion, looking for someone to devour") but didn't take it seriously. After a season of discouragement, I began feeling like I was in an old movie when a character has a little red devil sitting on one shoulder and an angel on the other. I could almost hear my enemy whispering: "give up, go home, you aren't good enough, you don't belong here." I would have to physically shake off the devil and start quoting Scripture to break the spell.

Here's a modern version of that verse in context.

1 Peter 5:8-11 (The Message)

[8-11] Keep a cool head. Stay alert. The Devil is poised to pounce, and would like nothing better than to catch you napping. Keep your guard up. You're not the only ones plunged into these hard times. It's the same with Christians all over the world. So keep a firm grip on the faith. The suffering won't last forever. It won't be long before this generous God who has great plans for us in Christ—eternal and glorious plans they are!—will have you put together and on your feet for good. He gets the last word; yes, he does.

POINTS TO PONDER:

There's a saying I love. It says, "Be the kind of woman that when your feet hit the floor each morning, the devil says, 'Oh crap, she's up!'"

What is one tactic the enemy uses to pester you? Write down part of one of the verses above to shout back at the devil before you get out of bed.

_____

_____

PRAYER:

Jehovah Chereb, the Lord, the Sword, remind me daily that You are here to help me fight my battles. I am not alone.

29
God Takes Action

"No matter what storm you face, you need to know that God loves you. He has not abandoned you."

- Franklin Graham

The good news is that we are not expected to engage in spiritual warfare all by ourselves. God gets involved and reacts in a big way when His beloved (that's YOU) is threatened. Read the following Psalm. What is the Lord's first response when He hears your cry of distress?

Psalm 18

[1] I love you, Lord;
you are my strength.
[2] The Lord is my rock, my fortress, and my savior;
my God is my rock, in whom I find protection.
He is my shield, the power that saves me,
and my place of safety.
[3] I called on the Lord, who is worthy of praise,
and he saved me from my enemies.

[4] The ropes of death entangled me;
floods of destruction swept over me.
[5] The grave wrapped its ropes around me;
death laid a trap in my path.
[6] But in my distress I cried out to the Lord;
yes, I prayed to my God for help.
He heard me from his sanctuary;
my cry to him reached his ears.
[7] Then the earth quaked and trembled.
The foundations of the mountains shook;
they quaked because of his anger.
[8] Smoke poured from his nostrils;
fierce flames leaped from his mouth.
Glowing coals blazed forth from him.
[9] He opened the heavens and came down;
dark storm clouds were beneath his feet.
[10] Mounted on a mighty angelic being, he flew,
soaring on the wings of the wind.
[11] He shrouded himself in darkness,
veiling his approach with dark rain clouds.
[12] Thick clouds shielded the brightness around him
and rained down hail and burning coals.
[13] The Lord thundered from heaven;
the voice of the Most High resounded
amid the hail and burning coals.

> ¹⁴ He shot his arrows and scattered his enemies;
> great bolts of lightning flashed, and they were confused.
> ¹⁵ Then at your command, O Lord,
> at the blast of your breath,
> the bottom of the sea could be seen,
> and the foundations of the earth were laid bare.
> ¹⁶ He reached down from heaven and rescued me;
> he drew me out of deep waters.
> ¹⁷ He rescued me from my powerful enemies,
> from those who hated me and were too strong for me.
> ¹⁸ They attacked me at a moment when I was in distress,
> but the Lord supported me.
> ¹⁹ He led me to a place of safety;
> he rescued me because he delights in me.

Talk about a superhero! What action does God take against the enemy? How does His behavior make you feel? What is the end result for you?

Meditate on the following passage that describes the victory we are promised.

Deuteronomy 20:1-4

> ¹ "When you go out to fight your enemies and you face horses and chariots and an army greater than your own, do not be afraid. The Lord your God, who brought you out of the land of Egypt, is with you! ² When you prepare for battle, the priest must come forward to speak to the troops. ³ He will say to them, 'Listen to me, all you men of Israel! Do not be afraid as you go out to fight your enemies today! Do not lose heart or panic or tremble before them. ⁴ For the Lord your God is going with you! He will fight for you against your enemies, and he will give you victory!'

I have been talking about God taking action against our enemies. But truthfully, the greatest message is that He is constantly on our side. I find the following passages incredibly valuable.

> During a British conference on comparative religions, experts from around the world debated what, if any, belief was unique to the Christian faith. They began eliminating possibilities. Incarnation? Other religions had different versions of gods appearing in human form. Resurrection? Again, other religions

had accounts of return from death. The debate went on for some time until C.S. Lewis wandered into the room. "What's the rumpus about?" he asked, and heard in reply that his colleagues were discussing Christianity's unique contribution among world religion. Lewis responded, "Oh that's easy. It's grace."

After some discussion, the conferees had to agree. The notion of God's love coming to us free of charge, no strings attached, seems to go against every instinct of humanity. The Buddhist eight-fold path, the Hindu doctrine of *karma*, the Jewish covenant, and Muslim code of law—each of these offers a way to earn approval. Only Christianity dares to make God's love unconditional.[34]

POINTS TO PONDER:

Even if you are not an artist, try drawing Psalm 18. What does God descending from heaven with smoke pouring from his nostrils and storm clouds beneath His feet look like?

PRAYER:

You are my Rock, my Fortress, my Shield. All I have to do is call on You, and You are by my side.

30
Poor Choices

"A lady's imagination is very rapid: It jumps from admiration to love, from love to matrimony in a moment."

- Jane Austen

As you read the following story, list how you relate to the woman who is described here.

John 4:1-26

4 Jesus knew the Pharisees had heard that he was baptizing and making more disciples than John ² (though Jesus himself didn't baptize them—his disciples did). ³ So he left Judea and returned to Galilee.

⁴ He had to go through Samaria on the way. ⁵ Eventually he came to the Samaritan village of Sychar, near the field that Jacob gave to his son Joseph. ⁶ Jacob's well was there; and Jesus, tired from the long walk, sat wearily beside the well about noontime. ⁷ Soon a Samaritan woman came to draw water, and Jesus said to her, "Please give me a drink." ⁸ He was alone at the time because his disciples had gone into the village to buy some food.

⁹ The woman was surprised, for Jews refuse to have anything to do with Samaritans. She said to Jesus, "You are a Jew, and I am a Samaritan woman. Why are you asking me for a drink?"

¹⁰ Jesus replied, "If you only knew the gift God has for you and who you are speaking to, you would ask me, and I would give you living water."

¹¹ "But sir, you don't have a rope or a bucket," she said, "and this well is very deep. Where would you get this living water? ¹² And besides, do you think you're greater than our ancestor Jacob, who gave us this well? How can you offer better water than he and his sons and his animals enjoyed?"

¹³ Jesus replied, "Anyone who drinks this water will soon become thirsty again. ¹⁴ But those who drink the water I give will never be thirsty again. It becomes a fresh, bubbling spring within them, giving them eternal life."

¹⁵ "Please, sir," the woman said, "give me this water! Then I'll never be thirsty again, and I won't have to come here to get water."

¹⁶ "Go and get your husband," Jesus told her.

[17] "I don't have a husband," the woman replied.

Jesus said, "You're right! You don't have a husband— [18] for you have had five husbands, and you aren't even married to the man you're living with now. You certainly spoke the truth!"

[19] "Sir," the woman said, "you must be a prophet. [20] So tell me, why is it that you Jews insist that Jerusalem is the only place of worship, while we Samaritans claim it is here at Mount Gerizim, where our ancestors worshiped?"

[21] Jesus replied, "Believe me, dear woman, the time is coming when it will no longer matter whether you worship the Father on this mountain or in Jerusalem. [22] You Samaritans know very little about the one you worship, while we Jews know all about him, for salvation comes through the Jews. [23] But the time is coming—indeed it's here now—when true worshipers will worship the Father in spirit and in truth. The Father is looking for those who will worship him that way. [24] For God is Spirit, so those who worship him must worship in spirit and in truth."

[25] The woman said, "I know the Messiah is coming—the one who is called Christ. When he comes, he will explain everything to us."

[26] Then Jesus told her, "I AM the Messiah!"

You most likely have not been married five times, but there's a good chance you've had a few relationships with men that have not worked out.

I dated a guy for eight months, and we talked about marriage. When he broke up with me, I was devastated. I think it was Rick Warren who said, "God sometimes removes a person from your life for your protection. Don't run after them."

I was particularly afraid that I wouldn't handle it as a "good Christian" and that my credibility would suffer since I was leading a singles' group at the time.

Below is my journal entry.

I still have to ask myself, "Do I believe God is who He says He is? Can I trust His promises? Can I live up to the standards I've been spouting all these years as a leader?" Even when he was pulling away, God gave me a verse: "For no matter how many promises God has made, they are Yes in Christ." He began preparing me even then to get my contentment and satisfaction and joy from Him and not have too high of expectations of my boyfriend. I didn't learn that lesson. In fact, I think for me at least it will be a life-long process. But I put it up on my closet door, and it's a daily reminder of my goal. Jesus *is* the answer to all my needs.

What are some reasons the woman was at the well at noon? Why is no one else there?

Have you ever lost a friendship because of the poor choices you've made?

How does Jesus begin His conversation with the Samaritan? What is unusual about that?

What does Jesus offer her?

How does Jesus get the woman to talk about her relationships? Why do you think He doesn't begin with that topic?

What are some reasons that could explain the woman's five marriages?

Looking back on your own past relationships, can you see a pattern in the type of man that attracts you? Is it a healthy pattern or does it need to be changed?

In my experience, the last two boyfriends I had before getting married were both extremely charismatic, life-of-the-party guys. I was attracted by their zest for life and their big dreams. I allowed myself to get swept up in their fast-paced world, and I ignored the warning signs. Believe it or not, one of the men had actually been married five times, like the Samaritan woman. I buried that enormous red flag! The other told me up front that he was in love with his first ex-wife (he had two) but thought I was the woman to cure him. Neither man treated me as valuable. Both were seeing other women behind my back. One said that all he wanted was for me to treat him like a king. When I began dating my husband, he said that he wanted to treat me like a queen for the rest of my life. Hmm... not really a hard decision to go with door number 3!

Ladies: You and I both know that women live their lives in the context of relationships. The challenge is to not cling so tightly that we suffocate the very thing we want so badly. We have to learn to relinquish our dependency on the relationship and the need to be needed. Otherwise, like the woman at the well and my ex-boyfriend, it is possible to go through one relationship after another without ever being satisfied.

Here are some ideas to ponder before dating.

1. Why him? How is he similar to the last guy I dated?
2. Am I at peace with myself?
3. Does he treat me with respect?
4. Am I driven by fear? You may fear that this is your last chance or that you are getting older and your biological clock is ticking.
5. Am I mistaking infatuation for love?
6. Do I need to be needed?
7. Why am I dating? Do I expect him to solve my loneliness or feelings of inadequacy?
8. Am I turning to the wrong source when it's living water I crave? If I was spiritually satisfied, would I want this relationship? To paraphrase Mark Jobe, "Thirsty people will drink muddy water."

When my boyfriend broke up with me, I went through a lot of anger and depression. My friends helped to keep me occupied, but they had busy lives and couldn't fill that hole. I realized how much I missed not just dating but having a *friend* that was devoted to me.

In my journal, I wrote the following passage.

Jesus spoke very clearly to me and said that He could be my best friend. It sounds so simple—like a kindergarten Sunday

School lesson—but it was profound to me. He went down the list of qualifications that He could bring to our friendship. He's always willing to go places with me. He'll always listen and be supportive. He'll always respond appropriately. He'll always love me and never stop communicating with me and never walk away. I tried it one morning. Jesus and I went on a walk up to the canyon before work. It wasn't an intense prayer time; it was just like I'd brought a friend with me, and we didn't feel the need to talk much.

A personal note about living water: When I was growing up, I had a mental image of myself as a well of fresh spring water. Anyone who needed refreshing could come to me and be satisfied. When my little brother would get in trouble or my parents would fight, I would draw on this source of peace to try to bring harmony into my home. It was not my job as a little girl, but that's what I thought I should be doing. During my first year of college, my dad left us for another woman. I had only been a Christian for nine months. I was frantic and depressed and overwhelmed. I knew I should be turning to the Word for consolation, but I had no idea how to find help in the Bible. Luckily, our Lord understands His young believers, and He very graciously "randomly" led me to John 4. When I read John 4:14 about Jesus providing living water, I knew that He knew all about me trying to be the well for my family. He showed me that I still could be the well, but that the strength and nourishment would be from Him alone. It was the first time I really understood what a personal God we serve.

Ultimately, I ended up loving my stepmother intensely. She and dad were very happy, and I don't bear any grudges.

POINTS TO PONDER:

I challenge you to do some homework. Make a list of the qualifications you would like in a platonic friendship with a man. Then, search the New Testament to find examples of how Jesus exhibits these characteristics.

PRAYER:

Jesus, I thank You for being my faithful Friend. Help me learn wisdom as I seek out other friends, male and female.

31
JEALOUSY/ENVY

"Jealousy is the poison we drink while we wait for our enemy to die."

- AUTHOR UNKNOWN

I think that we tend to treat jealousy and envy too lightly. We joke about other women's bodies, their boyfriends, jobs, talents, and even spirituality, but this humor can hide real hurt.

Jealousy and envy are similar, but there is a different twist. Being jealous makes you think, "I have what she wants, and I'm afraid she'll take it." There is a lot of selfishness involved. Envy can be described as feeling discontent, and it is often accompanied by ill will. "I lack what I want and therefore am discontent because someone else has it." Envy leads us to daydream about how our life would be if our wishes were fulfilled. Both are rooted in insecurity. Remember what Eleanor Roosevelt says: "No one can make you feel inferior without your consent."

Read the following verses and make a list of the damage that these destructive emotions can cause.

1 Samuel 18:1-13

After David had finished talking with Saul, he met Jonathan, the king's son. There was an immediate bond between them, for Jonathan loved David. ² From that day on Saul kept David with him and wouldn't let him return home. ³ And Jonathan made a solemn pact with David, because he loved him as he loved himself. ⁴ Jonathan sealed the pact by taking off his robe and giving it to David, together with his tunic, sword, bow, and belt.

⁵ Whatever Saul asked David to do, David did it successfully. So Saul made him a commander over the men of war, an appointment that was welcomed by the people and Saul's officers alike.

⁶ When the victorious Israelite army was returning home after David had killed the Philistine, women from all the towns of Israel came out to meet King Saul. They sang and danced for joy with tambourines and cymbals. ⁷ This was their song:

> "Saul has killed his thousands,
> and David his ten thousands!"

⁸ This made Saul very angry. "What's this?" he said. "They credit David with ten thousands and me with only thousands.

Next they'll be making him their king!" ⁹ So from that time on Saul kept a jealous eye on David.

¹⁰ The very next day a tormenting spirit from God overwhelmed Saul, and he began to rave in his house like a madman. David was playing the harp, as he did each day. But Saul had a spear in his hand, ¹¹ and he suddenly hurled it at David, intending to pin him to the wall. But David escaped him twice.

¹² Saul was then afraid of David, for the Lord was with David and had turned away from Saul. ¹³ Finally, Saul sent him away and appointed him commander over 1,000 men, and David faithfully led his troops into battle.

Genesis 30:1-4

When Rachel saw that she wasn't having any children for Jacob, she became jealous of her sister. She pleaded with Jacob, "Give me children, or I'll die!"

² Then Jacob became furious with Rachel. "Am I God?" he asked. "He's the one who has kept you from having children!"

³ Then Rachel told him, "Take my maid, Bilhah, and sleep with her. She will bear children for me, and through her I can have a family, too." ⁴ So Rachel gave her servant, Bilhah, to Jacob as a wife, and he slept with her.

Genesis 4:2-12

When they grew up, Abel became a shepherd, while Cain cultivated the ground. ³ When it was time for the harvest, Cain presented some of his crops as a gift to the Lord. ⁴ Abel also brought a gift—the best portions of the firstborn lambs from his flock. The Lord accepted Abel and his gift, ⁵ but he did not accept Cain and his gift. This made Cain very angry, and he looked dejected.

⁶ "Why are you so angry?" the Lord asked Cain. "Why do you look so dejected? ⁷ You will be accepted if you do what is right. But if you refuse to do what is right, then watch out!

Sin is crouching at the door, eager to control you. But you must subdue it and be its master."

⁸ One day Cain suggested to his brother, "Let's go out into the fields." And while they were in the field, Cain attacked his brother, Abel, and killed him.

⁹ Afterward the Lord asked Cain, "Where is your brother? Where is Abel?"

"I don't know," Cain responded. "Am I my brother's guardian?"

¹⁰ But the Lord said, "What have you done? Listen! Your brother's blood cries out to me from the ground! ¹¹ Now you are cursed and banished from the ground, which has swallowed your brother's blood. ¹² No longer will the ground yield good crops for you, no matter how hard you work! From now on you will be a homeless wanderer on the earth."

Genesis 37:3-8; 18-20

³ Jacob loved Joseph more than any of his other children because Joseph had been born to him in his old age. So one day Jacob had a special gift made for Joseph—a beautiful robe. ⁴ But his brothers hated Joseph because their father loved him more than the rest of them. They couldn't say a kind word to him. ⁵ One night Joseph had a dream, and when he told his brothers about it, they hated him more than ever. ⁶ "Listen to this dream," he said. ⁷ "We were out in the field, tying up bundles of grain. Suddenly my bundle stood up, and your bundles all gathered around and bowed low before mine!"

⁸ His brothers responded, "So you think you will be our king, do you? Do you actually think you will reign over us?" And they hated him all the more because of his dreams and the way he talked about them.

¹⁸ When Joseph's brothers saw him coming, they recognized him in the distance. As he approached, they made plans to kill him. ¹⁹ "Here comes the dreamer!" they said. ²⁰ "Come on, let's kill him and throw him into one of these cisterns. We can tell our father, 'A wild animal has eaten him.' Then we'll see what becomes of his dreams!"

Romans 13:10-14

¹⁰ Love does no wrong to others, so love fulfills the requirements of God's law.

¹¹ This is all the more urgent, for you know how late it is; time is running out. Wake up, for our salvation is nearer now than when we first believed. ¹² The night is almost gone; the day of salvation will soon be here. So remove your dark deeds like dirty clothes, and put on the shining armor of right living. ¹³ Because we belong to the day, we must live decent lives for all to see. Don't participate in the darkness of wild parties and drunkenness, or in sexual promiscuity and immoral living, or in quarreling and jealousy. ¹⁴ Instead, clothe yourself with the presence of the Lord Jesus Christ. And don't let yourself think about ways to indulge your evil desires.

1 Corinthians 3:1-3

Dear brothers and sisters, when I was with you I couldn't talk to you as I would to spiritual people. I had to talk as though you belonged to this world or as though you were infants in Christ. ² I had to feed you with milk, not with solid food, because you weren't ready for anything stronger. And you still aren't ready, ³ for you are still controlled by your sinful nature. You are jealous of one another and quarrel with each other. Doesn't that prove you are controlled by your sinful nature? Aren't you living like people of the world?

Acts 13:44-45

⁴⁴ The following week almost the entire city turned out to hear them preach the word of the Lord. ⁴⁵ But when some of the Jews saw the crowds, they were jealous; so they slandered Paul and argued against whatever he said.

Proverbs 27:4

Anger is cruel, and wrath is like a flood, but jealousy is even more dangerous.

James 3:13-16

¹³ If you are wise and understand God's ways, prove it by living an honorable life, doing good works with the humility

that comes from wisdom. ¹⁴ But if you are bitterly jealous and there is selfish ambition in your heart, don't cover up the truth with boasting and lying. ¹⁵ For jealousy and selfishness are not God's kind of wisdom. Such things are earthly, unspiritual, and demonic. ¹⁶ For wherever there is jealousy and selfish ambition, there you will find disorder and evil of every kind.

People who are jealous or envious often feel that they are a failure or inferior to others. They look for faults in other people and rejoice at others' failures. Gossip is a natural result of this mentality. Someone who is struggling with these sins will probably have a hard time feeling joyful or content.

This is a hard topic to face, but it is something we all must face. What areas of your life make you feel jealous or envious? What can you do to combat these feelings?

POINTS TO PONDER:

Which of the stories in this chapter did you relate to the most?

_____

In what area of your life are you most likely to suffer from jealousy or envy?

_____

PRAYER:

One of Your names is El Qanna, Jealous God. It overwhelms me that You desire such an intimate relationship with me that You actually get jealous when my attention is diverted from what is best for me. Help me conquer the worldly aspect of jealousy.

32
Running Away

"When written in Chinese, the word 'crisis' is composed of two characters. One represents danger and the other represents opportunity."

- John F. Kennedy

We have probably all run away from our problems in one way or another. Some of us may run to the fridge or a wine glass or the television. This is the story of a troubled woman who literally ran away.

Genesis 16:1-12

Now Sarai, Abram's wife, had not been able to bear children for him. But she had an Egyptian servant named Hagar. ² Sarai said to Abram, "The Lord has prevented me from having children. Go and sleep with my servant. Perhaps I can have children through her." And Abram agreed with Sarai's proposal. ³ So Sarai, Abram's wife, took Hagar the Egyptian servant and gave her to Abram as a wife. (This happened ten years after Abram had settled in the land of Canaan.)

⁴ So Abram had sexual relations with Hagar, and she became pregnant. But when Hagar knew she was pregnant, she began to treat her mistress, Sarai, with contempt. ⁵ Then Sarai said to Abram, "This is all your fault! I put my servant into your arms, but now that she's pregnant she treats me with contempt. The Lord will show who's wrong—you or me!"

⁶ Abram replied, "Look, she is your servant, so deal with her as you see fit." Then Sarai treated Hagar so harshly that she finally ran away.

⁷ The angel of the Lord found Hagar beside a spring of water in the wilderness, along the road to Shur. ⁸ The angel said to her, "Hagar, Sarai's servant, where have you come from, and where are you going?"

"I'm running away from my mistress, Sarai," she replied.

⁹ The angel of the Lord said to her, "Return to your mistress, and submit to her authority." ¹⁰ Then he added, "I will give you more descendants than you can count."

¹¹ And the angel also said, "You are now pregnant and will give birth to a son. You are to name him Ishmael (which means 'God hears'), for the Lord has heard your cry of distress. ¹² This son of yours will be a wild man, as untamed as a wild donkey! He will raise his fist against everyone, and

everyone will be against him. Yes, he will live in open hostility against all his relatives."

Do you feel sympathy or scorn for Hagar at the beginning of this story? Do those feelings change?

Have you ever run away? Remember that you can run away literally but also figuratively, trying to hide from a problem.

I hate to admit it, but I actually ran away once. I was a freshman in college, and my friends had hurt my feelings. Now, many years have passed, and I don't remember the exact circumstances. I just remember running blindly through the city, crying and hurt. By the time I stopped running, I wasn't even sure how to get back to campus. I think that's how Hagar feels, hurt and betrayed and unsure where to turn. That's where God meets her. Isn't He incredible?

How do you think Hagar saw herself when she got pregnant?

What might Hagar have been feeling when she ran away?

Why do you think the Lord told Hagar to return to Sarai? Can you think of a time when you had to swallow your pride?

I love that instead of allowing Hagar to feel sorry for herself, God points her toward the future. Do you think Hagar expected her son to become such a powerful person?

I imagine Hagar leaving Abram's camp that morning without a plan. She's pregnant and alone in a desert environment, most likely without sufficient food or water. I think the angel of the Lord (this phrase probably means Jesus) led her to that spring of refreshing water before revealing Himself. Now that she's had an encounter with God, Hagar doesn't have to run anymore. She can take refuge in Him.

Psalm 31:3-5 (The Message)

You're my cave to hide in,
my cliff to climb.
Be my safe leader,
be my true mountain guide.
Free me from hidden traps;
I want to hide in you.

> I've put my life in your hands.
> You won't drop me,
> you'll never let me down.

We may not literally leave our homes, but any time we turn away from God and turn toward another solution, we are running away spiritually.

> Isaiah 30:1-5
>
> [1] "What sorrow awaits my rebellious children,"
> says the Lord.
> "You make plans that are contrary to mine.
> You make alliances not directed by my Spirit,
> thus piling up your sins.
> [2] For without consulting me,
> you have gone down to Egypt for help.
> You have put your trust in Pharaoh's protection.
> You have tried to hide in his shade.
> [3] But by trusting Pharaoh, you will be humiliated,
> and by depending on him, you will be disgraced.
> [4] For though his power extends to Zoan
> and his officials have arrived in Hanes,
> [5] all who trust in him will be ashamed.
> He will not help you.
> Instead, he will disgrace you."

Can you hear the pain in God's voice? He knows the outcome when we "make plans that are contrary" to His because He is always on our side.

POINTS TO PONDER:

Which part of Hagar's story reminds you of yourself? How will you react the next time you want to run away from a problem?

PRAYER:

I thank You, Lord Jesus, that even when I try to escape, You find me and bring me to a place of refreshment and encouragement with a healthy dose of honesty.

33
Fully Known

"Always be a first-rate version of yourself, instead of a second-rate version of somebody else."

- Judy Garland

One of the reasons people look forward to heaven is having their questions answered. 1 Corinthians 13:12 says, "For now we see only a reflection as in a mirror; then we shall see face to face. Now I know in part; then I shall know fully." As exciting as that promise is, the rest of the verse has an even greater impact on me. God assures me that I shall know fully "even as I am fully known."

Like many, I struggle to completely accept God's unconditional love for me. But even more amazing is understanding that He knows me inside and out and still loves me. Even as a happily married woman, I am not "fully known" by my husband or anyone else on this earth.

Let's continue Hagar's adventure.

Genesis 16:13-16

[13] Thereafter, Hagar used another name to refer to the Lord, who had spoken to her. She said, "You are the God who sees me." She also said, "Have I truly seen the One who sees me?" [14] So that well was named Beer-lahai-roi (which means "well of the Living One who sees me"). It can still be found between Kadesh and Bered.

[15] So Hagar gave Abram a son, and Abram named him Ishmael. [16] Abram was eighty-six years old when Ishmael was born.

What is significant about the name Hagar gives God? Think of a time in your own life when you felt fully known by God.

My favorite personal example is when I was living in San Diego and going through a financial crisis. I was between jobs and on unemployment, and it wasn't enough. I couldn't pay my rent, and I was starting to panic. One day, I received an envelope in the mail that was postmarked Nazareth, TX. I didn't know anyone in Texas. Inside were two checks totaling $555 — enough to cover my rent. But the best part was a typewritten note that read "The Man of Nazareth is proud of you." I wish you could have seen my happy dance. To think that Jesus wrote me a letter! I'm sure that someone from my church arranged it, but God orchestrated the miracle. He is creative, and He knows what you need.

What does Hagar say after she names God? Say this for yourself. What do you feel?

How does this encounter help Hagar to return?

This is a story of grace. Hagar was probably an idol worshiper and not a seeker, yet our God seeks those who are lost.

Ezekiel 34:11-16

[11] "For this is what the Sovereign Lord says: I myself will search and find my sheep. [12] I will be like a shepherd looking for his scattered flock. I will find my sheep and rescue them from all the places where they were scattered on that dark and cloudy day. [13] I will bring them back home to their own land of Israel from among the peoples and nations. I will feed them on the mountains of Israel and by the rivers and in all the places where people live. [14] Yes, I will give them good pastureland on the high hills of Israel. There they will lie down in pleasant places and feed in the lush pastures of the hills. [15] I myself will tend my sheep and give them a place to lie down in peace, says the Sovereign Lord. [16] I will search for my lost ones who strayed away, and I will bring them safely home again. I will bandage the injured and strengthen the weak. But I will destroy those who are fat and powerful. I will feed them, yes—feed them justice!

Jeremiah 23:1-4

[1] "What sorrow awaits the leaders of my people—the shepherds of my sheep—for they have destroyed and scattered the very ones they were expected to care for," says the Lord.

[2] Therefore, this is what the Lord, the God of Israel, says to these shepherds: "Instead of caring for my flock and leading them to safety, you have deserted them and driven them to destruction. Now I will pour out judgment on you for the evil you have done to them. [3] But I will gather together the remnant of my flock from the countries where I have driven them. I will bring them back to their own sheepfold, and they will be fruitful and increase in number. [4] Then I will appoint responsible shepherds who will care for them, and

they will never be afraid again. Not a single one will be lost or missing. I, the Lord, have spoken!

When you have "Hagar times" and feel injured or weak, focus on the verses above.

There are infinite things about our Almighty God that astound me, but one of the most profound is how well He knows me. As a single woman, I remember hungering for a relationship with someone who really "got" me. I was always sending out long emails to friends in an effort to be fully known. I am doing it now by writing this book! Now I know that I have always had a relationship where I was fully known. God has known me since before conception.

Psalm 139:1-6; 13-18

[1] O Lord, you have examined my heart
and know everything about me.
[2] You know when I sit down or stand up.
You know my thoughts even when I'm far away.
[3] You see me when I travel
and when I rest at home.
You know everything I do.
[4] You know what I am going to say
even before I say it, Lord.
[5] You go before me and follow me.
You place your hand of blessing on my head.
[6] Such knowledge is too wonderful for me,
too great for me to understand!

[13] You made all the delicate, inner parts of my body
and knit me together in my mother's womb.
[14] Thank you for making me so wonderfully complex!
Your workmanship is marvelous—how well I know it.
[15] You watched me as I was being formed in utter seclusion,
as I was woven together in the dark of the womb.
[16] You saw me before I was born.
Every day of my life was recorded in your book.
Every moment was laid out
before a single day had passed.

[17] How precious are your thoughts about me, O God.

They cannot be numbered!
¹⁸ I can't even count them;
they outnumber the grains of sand!
And when I wake up,
you are still with me!

Jeremiah 12:3a

But as for me, Lord, you know my heart. You see me and test my thoughts.

John 10:27

My sheep listen to my voice; I know them, and they follow me.

Psalm 31:7

I will be glad and rejoice in your unfailing love,
for you have seen my troubles,
and you care about the anguish of my soul.

Some of the above verses demonstrate that God's intimate knowledge of you is not always comfortable. Is there anything in these verses that makes you uneasy? Why is that?

Having our darkest thoughts exposed is risky.

Hebrews 4:13

Nothing in all creation is hidden from God. Everything is naked and exposed before his eyes, and he is the one to whom we are accountable.

Matthew 10:26

But don't be afraid of those who threaten you. For the time is coming when everything that is covered will be revealed, and all that is secret will be made known to all.

Luke 16:15

Then he said to them, "You like to appear righteous in public, but God knows your hearts. What this world honors is detestable in the sight of God."

Being vulnerable can be scary, but remember that it's better than going back into slavery.

Galatians 4:8-9

[8] Before you Gentiles knew God, you were slaves to so-called gods that do not even exist. [9] So now that you know God (or should I say, now that God knows you), why do you want to go back again and become slaves once more to the weak and useless spiritual principles of this world?

The wonderful news is that not only does God know us, but He is willing for us to know Him. Spend a few moments contemplating this amazing fact.

Numbers 12:6-8a

[6] And the Lord said to them, "Now listen to what I say:
"If there were prophets among you,
I, the Lord, would reveal myself in visions.
I would speak to them in dreams.
[7] But not with my servant Moses.
Of all my house, he is the one I trust.
[8] I speak to him face to face,
clearly, and not in riddles!
He sees the Lord as he is.

Whose opinion do you tend to believe when it comes to your value?

> "I know that my self-image at the end of the day depends largely on what kind of messages I have received from other people. Am I liked? Am I loved? I await the answers from my friends, my neighbors, my family—like a starving man I await the answers."[35]

Do you find yourself listening to negative comments? How can we see ourselves honestly?

Read the following verses for some help answering the questions above.

1 Corinthians 4:3-4

As for me, it matters very little how I might be evaluated by you or by any human authority. I don't even trust my own judgment on this point. My conscience is clear, but that doesn't prove I'm right. It is the Lord himself who will examine me and decide.

Romans 12:3

Because of the privilege and authority God has given me, I give each of you this warning: Don't think you are better than you really are. Be honest in your evaluation of yourselves, measuring yourselves by the faith God has given us.

1 Peter 5:5-7 (The Message)

be down to earth with each other, for—God has had it with the proud,
But takes delight in just plain people.

So be content with who you are, and don't put on airs. God's strong hand is on you; he'll promote you at the right time. Live carefree before God; he is most careful with you.

Just like Hagar and Paul, you can think whatever you want about yourself, but that doesn't make it right. The God Who Sees knows exactly who you are and what you need. On my mission trip to Scotland with YWAM, we set up our drama/evangelism team next to a church group with a pastor who was preaching a strong message against sin. He said something about sin being a cancer. Suddenly, a man in the audience began yelling and crying. People tried to talk to him, but he broke free. Later, we learned that he ran straight into a man on the corner wearing a large sandwich board proclaiming the end of times. Truthfully, the YWAM team thought this preacher was sort of obnoxious and didn't approve of his methods. This "fanatic" ended up counseling the man and found out that the man's wife had died from cancer. The cancer reference in the sermon broke him. The God Who Sees knew what this man needed and whom he needed it from. He often works in a way we least expect. Can you think of a time when things turned out differently than you had anticipated?

POINTS TO PONDER:

Like my "Man from Nazareth" story, write down a time when you know that God was watching. It doesn't have to be dramatic, just a clear instance to return to when you feel lost.

_____

_____

_____

PRAYER:

Here I am Lord, warts and all. It is intimidating to consider how deeply You know me, and yet, it is also comforting. Today, I want to do nothing but sit in Your presence and soak in Your love.

34
HE DELIGHTS IN YOU

"He led me to a place of safety; he rescued me because he delights in me."

- 2 SAMUEL 22:20

If this verse doesn't make you think of a hero on a white horse then I don't know what will. Jesus wants to rescue **YOU**, His precious maiden. After all, "You will be called Sought After, the City No Longer Deserted" (Isaiah 62:12 NIV).

So, what do you think God notices when He sees you as He saw Hagar? To name just a few things, He recognizes that you are:

Psalm 4:3 (Living Bible)

The Lord has set apart the *redeemed* for himself. Therefore he will listen to me and answer when I call to him.

Isaiah 62:12 (NIV)

They will be called the *Holy People*,
the Redeemed of the Lord;
and you will be called *Sought After,*
the City No Longer Deserted.

Isaiah 58:12 (NIV)

Your people will rebuild the ancient ruins
and will raise up the age-old foundations;
you will be called *Repairer of Broken Walls,*
Restorer of Streets with Dwellings.

Deuteronomy 26:18-19

[18] The Lord has declared today that you are his people, *his own special treasure*, just as he promised, and that you must obey all his commands. [19] And if you do, he will set you high above all the other nations he has made. Then you will receive praise, honor, and renown. You will be a nation that is holy to the Lord your God, just as he promised.

Deuteronomy 7:6

For you are a *holy people*, who belong to the Lord your God. Of all the people on earth, the Lord your God has chosen you to be his own special treasure.

Ephesians 1:4-5 (NIV)

For *he chose us in him* before the creation of the world to be holy and blameless in his sight. In love he predestined us for adoption to sonship through Jesus Christ, in accordance with his pleasure and will.

Were you a jock in school, or do you remember being chosen last for softball, like me? God <u>chose</u> to adopt you, not just because He loves you in the sense that "God loves the whole world" but because He likes you and wants to spend time with you. I think if we understood this concept, it would change our lives.

Pastor Mark Jobe told the following story. A five-year-old boy had a new baby brother, and he kept staring at him. Finally, he asked, "Does he know who he is or does he just lie there and think he's nothing?" Knowing who we are makes all the difference in the world. Many Christians know in their heads Whose they are, but they don't live like that.

<u>1 John 3:1-3</u> (NIV)

See what great love the Father has lavished on us, that we should be called children of God! And that is what we are! The reason the world does not know us is that it did not know him. ² Dear friends, now we are children of God, and what we will be has not yet been made known. But we know that when Christ appears, we shall be like him, for we shall see him as he is. ³ All who have this hope in him purify themselves, just as he is pure.

How does the word "lavished" make you feel?

Have you ever had a reputation about yourself already established before meeting someone new? Maybe you had a sibling who excelled in sports, and the coach expected the same from you, or a neighbor judged you because of your skin color or income level.

I have a positive example of being labeled. I moved to the town where my dad lived and attended a party at his house. Everyone I met said, "Oh you're *Larry's* daughter." I could tell this was high praise indeed. I was practically glowing by the end of the day because I got to introduce myself as the relative of a highly regarded person. That night, the Lord oh so gently nudged me and asked, "Are you that proud of being *My* daughter?" (See the appendix for a song I wrote years later on this same subject called *My Father's Voice*.)

Meditate on verse 2. Which phrase is the most meaningful to you?

Pastor Jobe preached that there are many unfinished paintings by Michelangelo. You can see hands and faces beginning to emerge into a masterpiece. Our Daddy is an artist too, who makes us like Him.

Why is this concept important? If you truly got it into your heart that you are a child of the Father God who lavishes love upon you, what might change in your earthly relationships?

It is my strong hope that implanting this verse in your heart will mean no more abusive relationships, no more dating jerks just to have a man in your life, no more accepting the lie that you aren't worth the love and respect you have the right to expect. An old African proverb says: If you don't know who you are or you don't know your name, then anybody can name you.

Cute story alert: Another young grandson was curious about my "real" name. He kept asking Bob, "What's Nana's name?" and Bob would teasingly reply, "Nana." My grandson kept asking in various ways until he finally said, "How does she sign her checks?" Bob was surprised, and our boy said, "I'm smarter than you think I am."

God named me, and my identity is found in Him. "The one who is in you is greater than the one who in the world" (I John 4:4 NIV).

The following is a love letter from God to you. All of it is Scripture, just rearranged and with some of the tenses altered. I did this as an exercise to remind myself how much God loves you and me.

Dear child:

I bring out the stars one by one and call them each by name. Because of My great power and mighty strength, not one of them is missing. I give orders to the morning and show the dawn its place. I bring forth the constellations in their seasons. I send the lightning bolts on their way. Who else is God beside Me? Who else is a Rock? I am your light and salvation. You have nothing to fear. I am your stronghold—

what could you fear? When you are afraid, trust in Me. What can mortal man do to you?

I made you—you are Mine! I created your inmost being. I knit you together in your mother's womb. All of your days are written in My book. I will remember My covenant with you. I take great delight in you. I will quiet you with My love. I rejoice over you with signing. Nothing can separate you from My love. My love for you surpasses knowledge.

I am close to you when you are broken-hearted. I save you when your spirit is crushed. I know your anxious thoughts, and I will lead you in the way everlasting. When anxiety is great within you, My consolation will bring joy to your soul. When you are in distress, seek Me. Remember Me and think about the former days. I am a God who performs miracles. Consider all My mighty works. I will give strength to you when you are weary and increase your power when you are weak. I hear you when you cry and lift you out of the slimy pit. I will deliver your soul from death, your eyes from tears, and your feet from stumbling. Come to Me when you are weary and burdened, and I will give you rest. Approach My throne of grace with confidence and you will receive mercy and grace to help you. I, too, was tempted and can sympathize with your weaknesses.

I will not reject your prayers or withhold My love from you. I will not hide My face from you. When you cry to Me I hear your voice. Call to Me and I will answer you. Put your trust in Me and hide in Me. I will teach you to do My will. I will lead you on level ground. I will make your steps firm. Though you stumble, you will not fall, for I uphold you with My hand. I put your feet on a rock and give you a firm place to stand. I will teach you My ways so that you can walk in My truth. I am your hiding place. I will surround you with songs of deliverance. I am your rock, your fortress, and your deliverer. You will find rest in Me alone. You will never be shaken. I arm you with strength. I give you My shield of victory. My right hand sustains you. I broaden the path beneath you.

Put your hope in My word, for My love is unfailing—it surrounds you. Forget the former things; do not dwell on the past. See, I am doing a new thing! What I have said, that will I bring about; what I have planned, that I will do. For I know the plans that I have for you—plans for a future and a hope. Be fully persuaded that I have the power to do what I have promised. I will teach you wondrous things that you do not know. You are more than a conqueror because of My love for you. I am faithful. I will complete the good work I began in you.

Like clay in the hands of the potter, so are you in My hands. I shape you as seems best to Me. I will test you and refine you like silver. You will go through fire and water but you will come to a place of abundance. I am bringing you into a good land. I have been with you wherever you have gone. Be strong and courageous. Be careful to obey My words. Do not be terrified, do not be discouraged, for I will be with you wherever you go.

I do not look at the things man looks at. Man looks at outward appearance, but I look at the heart. Your labor in My work is not in vain. Do not lose heart. You are My ambassador. You are being transformed into My likeness with every increasing glory. Do not be weary in doing good, for you will reap a harvest glory if you do not give up. Your confidence will be richly rewarded. Run your race with perseverance! After you have done My will, you will receive all that I have promised. Hold unswervingly to your hope, for I am faithful. Your light and momentary troubles are achieving an eternal glory for you that far outweighs them all. I can do immeasurably more than you could ask or even imagine. That power is at work in you. You can do anything with My strength.

Fix your eyes on the eternal. You are blessed! You are invited to My wedding supper! In the new Jerusalem, there will be no more death or mourning or crying or pain. I will wipe every tear from your eye. There will be no more night. You will not need a lamp, for I will give you light. You will see My face and know Me as I already fully know you. My words are trustworthy and true. I do not lie. I am coming soon!

POINTS TO PONDER:

Take out your highlighter and mark the phrases that mean the most to you in the letter from God above. Meditate on one or two. Meditation isn't spooky. It just means mulling over something in your mind, concentrating on what it means, and letting it sink into your soul.

PRAYER:

My Rock, My Light, My Stronghold, I thank You for seeing the beauty in me that I cannot see.

35
Standing Firm

"When we long for life without difficulties, remind us that oaks grow strong in contrary winds, and diamonds are made under pressure."

- Peter Marshall

We've all heard the expression, "Don't just stand there, do something." But maybe we got it wrong.

> I think God is crying out and shouting to us: "Don't just do something. Stand there! Enter into a love relationship with Me. Get to know Me. Adjust your life to Me. Let Me love you and reveal Myself to you as I work through you."[36]

Consider the problem Jehoshaphat is facing below.

<u>2 Chronicles 20:1-4</u>

> [1] After this, the armies of the Moabites, Ammonites, and some of the Meunites declared war on Jehoshaphat. [2] Messengers came and told Jehoshaphat, "A vast army from Edom is marching against you from beyond the Dead Sea. They are already at Hazazon-tamar." (This was another name for En-gedi.) [3] Jehoshaphat was terrified by this news and begged the Lord for guidance. He also ordered everyone in Judah to begin fasting. [4] So people from all the towns of Judah came to Jerusalem to seek the Lord's help.

When have you felt as if your problems are multiplying so fast that you can't face them all?

What two things does Jehoshaphat do in response to his fear?

> I don't know about you, but I often get these steps in the wrong order. Instead of first asking God for guidance and then enlisting my friends' prayer support, I often turn to other people first.

<u>2 Chronicles 20:5-20</u>

> [5] Jehoshaphat stood before the community of Judah and Jerusalem in front of the new courtyard at the Temple of the Lord. [6] He prayed, "O Lord, God of our ancestors, you alone are the God who is in heaven. You are ruler of all the kingdoms of the earth. You are powerful and mighty; no one can stand against you! [7] O our God, did you not drive out those who lived in this land when your people Israel arrived? And did you not give this land forever to the descendants of your friend Abraham? [8] Your people settled here and built this Temple to honor your name. [9] They said, 'Whenever we are faced with

any calamity such as war, plague, or famine, we can come to stand in your presence before this Temple where your name is honored. We can cry out to you to save us, and you will hear us and rescue us.' ¹⁰ "And now see what the armies of Ammon, Moab, and Mount Seir are doing. You would not let our ancestors invade those nations when Israel left Egypt, so they went around them and did not destroy them. ¹¹ Now see how they reward us! For they have come to throw us out of your land, which you gave us as an inheritance. ¹² O our God, won't you stop them? We are powerless against this mighty army that is about to attack us. We do not know what to do, but we are looking to you for help."

Why does Jehoshaphat tell God things He already knows? Which of God's promises can you recite back to Him about your situation? If you can't think of any off the top of your head, perhaps one or more of the following fits your circumstances.

Psalm 34:17-19

The Lord hears his people when they call to him for help. He rescues them from all their troubles. The Lord is close to the brokenhearted; he rescues those whose spirits are crushed. The righteous person faces many troubles, but the Lord comes to the rescue each time.

Isaiah 43:1-2

¹ But now, O Jacob, listen to the Lord who created you.
O Israel, the one who formed you says,
"Do not be afraid, for I have ransomed you.
I have called you by name; you are mine.
² When you go through deep waters,
I will be with you.
When you go through rivers of difficulty,
you will not drown.
When you walk through the fire of oppression,
you will not be burned up;
the flames will not consume you.

Jeremiah 3:22

"My wayward children," says the Lord, "come back to me, and I will heal your wayward hearts."

Deuteronomy 4:29a

And if you search for him with all your heart and soul, you will find him.

Proverbs 11:25

The generous will prosper; those who refresh others will themselves be refreshed.

1 Corinthians 10:13

The temptations in your life are no different from what others experience. And God is faithful. He will not allow the temptation to be more than you can stand. When you are tempted, he will show you a way out so that you can endure.

Acts 3:19-20

[19] Now repent of your sins and turn to God, so that your sins may be wiped away. [20] Then times of refreshment will come from the presence of the Lord, and he will again send you Jesus, your appointed Messiah.

How would you describe Jehoshaphat's tone of voice? When was the last time you said something similar to verse 12?

2 Chronicles 20:13-17

[13] As all the men of Judah stood before the Lord with their little ones, wives, and children, [14] the Spirit of the Lord came upon one of the men standing there. His name was Jahaziel son of Zechariah, son of Benaiah, son of Jeiel, son of Mattaniah, a Levite who was a descendant of Asaph.

[15] He said, "Listen, all you people of Judah and Jerusalem! Listen, King Jehoshaphat! This is what the Lord says: Do not be afraid! Don't be discouraged by this mighty army, for the battle is not yours, but God's. [16] Tomorrow, march out against them. You will find them coming up through the ascent of Ziz at the end of the valley that opens into the wilderness of Jeruel. [17] But you will not even need to fight. Take your positions; then stand still and watch the Lord's victory. He is with you, O people of Judah and Jerusalem.

Do not be afraid or discouraged. Go out against them tomorrow, for the Lord is with you!"

What method does God use to answer the king's prayer?

I doubt that many people remember the name Jahaziel (I didn't). But don't you love it when God looks down and chooses one person to use mightily? Don't you wonder what Jahaziel's qualifications were? How do you suppose this man had lived so that he was open to the descent of the Holy Spirit upon him?

2 Chronicles 20:18-19

[18] Then King Jehoshaphat bowed low with his face to the ground. And all the people of Judah and Jerusalem did the same, worshiping the Lord. [19] Then the Levites from the clans of Kohath and Korah stood to praise the Lord, the God of Israel, with a very loud shout.

Imagine being one of the crowd listening to his instructions.

What different forms of worship are displayed? How do you use worship to fight the battles in your life? How could you use it more effectively?

2 Chronicles 20:20-21

[20] Early the next morning the army of Judah went out into the wilderness of Tekoa. On the way Jehoshaphat stopped and said, "Listen to me, all you people of Judah and Jerusalem! Believe in the Lord your God, and you will be able to stand firm. Believe in his prophets, and you will succeed."

[21] After consulting the people, the king appointed singers to walk ahead of the army, singing to the Lord and praising him for his holy splendor. This is what they sang:

"Give thanks to the Lord;
his faithful love endures forever!"

How do you think you would have responded to being told not to fight the mighty armies that were approaching?

Can you think of any situations in your life where fighting your problems through your own strength may have made them worse?

I directed a high school play and ran into some conflicts with parents about scheduling. After conversations where I was falsely accused of wrongdoing, I raised my voice in retaliation. Afterward, I felt sick to my stomach. I (finally) learned to let go of the need to defend myself, which meant I could just focus on my job. Verse 17 in the NIV says, "Take up your positions; stand firm and see the deliverance the Lord will give you." The Lord has so much to give us, but we often miss out because we are not in the right position, and we are not standing firm.

For me, the most difficult area to maintain a firm stance was keeping my virginity. I humbly confess to you, my sisters, that sexually, I strayed far more than I wish I had. But by stubbornly digging my heels into the Lord's promises, I managed to stay a virgin until my marriage at the age of 46. That's a semi-miracle in this day and age. If you are a virgin, I urge you to use these verses to help you stand firm in that decision. If you are not, be sure to spend time confessing that, but then accept God's forgiveness and vow to stay chaste from this time forward.

POINTS TO PONDER:

Choose one of the verses below to memorize this week. Don't pick the shortest one (got you), but the one that "zings" your heart when you read it. As you work on learning it by heart, consider which area of your life requires a firm stance.

2 Chronicles 20:15b (NLT)

Do not be afraid. Don't be discouraged by this mighty arm, for the battle is not yours, but God's.

Exodus 14:13a (Amplified Bible)

Moses told the people, Fear not; stand still (firm, confident, undismayed) and see the salvation of the Lord which He will work for you today.

Job 11:14-16 (NIV)

If you put away the sin that is in your hand and allow no evil to dwell in your tent, then, free of fault, you will lift up your face; you will stand firm and without fear. You will surely forget your trouble, recalling it only as waters gone by.

Proverbs 10:25 (The Message)

When the storm is over, there's nothing left of the wicked; good people, firm on their rock foundation, aren't even fazed.

1 Corinthians 1:7-9 (NIV)

Therefore you do not lack any spiritual gift as you eagerly wait for our Lord Jesus Christ to be revealed. He will also keep you firm to the end, so that you will be blameless on the day of our Lord Jesus Christ. God is faithful, who has called you into fellowship with his Son, Jesus Christ our Lord.

1 Corinthians 15:58 (NIV)

Therefore, my dear brothers and sisters, stand firm. Let nothing move you. Always give yourselves fully to the work of the Lord, because you know that your labor in the Lord is not in vain.

2 Corinthians 1:21-22 (NLT)

It is God who enables us, along with you, to stand firm for Christ. He has commissioned us, and he has identified us as his own by placing the Holy Spirit in our hearts as the first installment that guarantees everything he has promised us.

Galatians 5:1 (NIV)

It is for freedom that Christ has set us free. Stand firm, then, and do not let yourselves be burdened again by a yoke of slavery.

Ephesians 6:10-13 (NASB)

Finally, be strong in the Lord and in the strength of His might. Put on the full armor of God, so that you will be able to stand firm against the schemes of the devil. For our struggle is not against flesh and blood, but against the rulers, against the powers, against the world forces of this darkness, against the spiritual forces of wicked-ness in the heavenly places. Therefore, take up the full armor of God, so that you will be able to resist in the evil day, and having done everything, to stand firm.

2 Corinthians 2:15 (The Message)

So, friends, take a firm stand, feet on the ground and head high. Keep a tight grip on what you were taught, whether in personal conversation or by our letter. May Jesus himself and God our Father, who reached out in love and surprised you with gifts of unending help and confidence, put a fresh heart in you, invigorate your work, enliven your speech.

PRAYER:

Jesus, my shelter and my fortress, today I draw a line in the sand and plant my feet behind it. I tell the devil, "You are not coming one inch closer." Help me as I stand firm for Your kingdom.

36
FAILURE IS A FACT OF LIFE

"We are never defeated
unless we give up on God."

- RONALD REGAN

Abraham became my favorite Bible personality when I answered God's call to full-time missions. Granted, compared to Africa or China, Chicago felt relatively safe and familiar. Yet, at that time, I felt like I had no idea where I was going or what my life would become. At least Abraham took his family with him.

Hebrews 11:8-10 (The Living Bible)

> [8] Abraham trusted God, and when God told him to leave home and go far away to another land that he promised to give him, Abraham obeyed. Away he went, not even knowing where he was going. [9] And even when he reached God's promised land, he lived in tents like a mere visitor as did Isaac and Jacob, to whom God gave the same promise. [10] Abraham did this because he was confidently waiting for God to bring him to that strong heavenly city whose designer and builder is God.

I heard retreat speaker Judy Rachels, and her message prepared me for my move to Illinois to a certain extent. She said that we all like our comfort zones, like Archie Bunker's chair. But taking joy in the journey inevitably requires leaving: leaving the womb, leaving home, leaving singleness, leaving self-centeredness (parenting), leaving control (empty nest). Leaving is always painful.

I was completely alone, and I felt like a total outsider in my Mexican neighborhood. I had been an accomplished small group Bible study leader in San Diego, and I was oh so confident I could do the same job in this new church. But my pride quickly took a beating. My skill set for the big church on the hill filled with wealthy Protestant Caucasians did not match the blue collar, ex-gang member, ex-prostitute, Catholic congregation in my new environment. I had to drive all over town to pick up the women in my study, and then all they wanted to talk about was how bad their husbands were. (Of course, being single, they didn't get much sympathy from me!) Then, I drove them all home, exhausted and feeling like a total failure. Where was the ministry in this? Ms. Rachels told her audience that failure is a fact of life. If you think about it, even Jesus "failed" with the rich young ruler (Matthew 19:22). The son of God did not save Jerusalem (Matthew 23:37-39) and was unable to do His miracles in Nazareth (Mark 6:1-6). But failure is not final. Think of Peter betraying Jesus, surely the worst failure of all, and yet God used him to preach at Pentecost.

What does failure really mean? The following is an excerpt from my journal.

> The Lord is calling me to a place of surrender, and it's scary. I gave Him all my fears Friday night after a week of prayer meetings, and He basically confronted me with: "What's the worst that could happen?" Bankruptcy, spinsterhood, no ministry. . . and I realized that I could handle that if He didn't leave. I feel very dependent, which I'm sure was His goal from the start—like I can hardly get out of bed without Jesus.

At that moment, I realized that failing was not the end of the world. Like Thomas Edison says, "I have not failed. I've just found 10,000 ways that won't work." Losing faith, however, is devastating. Part of me is jealous of the 37-year-old Janan that needed Jesus to get out of bed. In reality, that is still true today, but we get comfortable and lose our awareness of our desperate need for Christ.

When you are tempted to give up, Satan has won. He isn't after your salvation—he lost a soul the moment you gave your heart to Jesus—but he can make you an ineffectual witness and keep you from spreading the good news.

Judy Rachels told a Chinese proverb.

> A father has one horse and one son. The horse ran away. The neighbors said, "Oh, that's bad." The father said, "How do you know?" The next day the horse reappeared leading a pack of wild horses. The neighbors said, "Oh, that's good." The father said, "How do you know?" The next day the son went out to break the horses and was thrown off. He ended up in the hospital with broken bones. The neighbors said, "Oh, that's bad." The father said, "How do you know?" The next day the warlord came and conscripted all the able-bodied young men to go to war from which they would never return but he did not take the son with the broken bones.

Like the parable above, my life makes perfect sense in hindsight. If I hadn't left San Diego to go to Chicago, I would have never moved to

Wisconsin. If I hadn't moved to Wisconsin, I would not have met my husband. If I hadn't been so frustrated leading Bible studies in Chicago, I would not have been so open/available to write an Easter play and become involved in drama ministry. That led to a regular drama ministry and a 20-year "hobby" of acting and directing in theater, television, and film. How do we know how God will turn our life around? Just like in the story of Joseph, people or the devil may be out to get you, but God is still in control.

Genesis 50:20

You intended to harm me, but God intended it all for good. He brought me to this position so I could save the lives of many people.

One amazing benefit of failure is that it equips you to minister much more effectively.

2 Corinthians 3:7

[3] All praise to God, the Father of our Lord Jesus Christ. God is our merciful Father and the source of all comfort. [4] He comforts us in all our troubles so that we can comfort others. When they are troubled, we will be able to give them the same comfort God has given us. [5] For the more we suffer for Christ, the more God will shower us with his comfort through Christ. [6] Even when we are weighed down with troubles, it is for your comfort and salvation! For when we ourselves are comforted, we will certainly comfort you. Then you can patiently endure the same things we suffer. [7] We are confident that as you share in our sufferings, you will also share in the comfort God gives us.

In other words, use your past mistakes! I dated so many wrong men, but now I can tell my stories to my granddaughters to hopefully shed some light for them about what to look for in a future spouse. If I was one of those lucky ones who married their high-school sweetheart, I wouldn't have these experiences to pass on.

Christian performer Kathy Troccoli spoke at a conference I attended. She testified to having suffered from low self-esteem, bulimia, depression, despair, loneliness, bankruptcy, friendship betrayal, and being single! Kathy has reached thousands of women with her story and knows how God can use your past hurts to encourage others. But she says the danger is that so many women keep wearing their grave clothes wrapped around them tightly after God has set them free. We get one arm out and maybe a leg and think that's enough. The world is not going to be impressed with our deliverance if we are still limping around.

POINTS TO PONDER:

"Abraham obeyed. Away he went, not even knowing where he was going." Are you in a similar situation, feeling unsure of what is around the corner? Abraham "was fully convinced that God is able to do whatever he promises" (Romans 4:21).

Write down your fears about the future. Now, take some time to research promises in the Bible that will encourage you. If this is new for you, try using the concordance in the back of your Bible or online.

PRAYER:

Jehovah Shalom, The Lord our Peace, remind me that You are in control. Give me a greater trust in Your plan and bring me peace of heart.

37
GO HOME!

"Worry implies that we don't quite trust God is big enough, powerful enough, or loving enough to take care of what's happening in our lives."

- FRANCIS CHAN

The Old Testament includes a list of battle regulations for the Israelites.

Deuteronomy 20:5-8

⁵"Then the officers of the army must address the troops and say, 'Has anyone here just built a new house but not yet dedicated it? If so, you may go home! You might be killed in the battle, and someone else would dedicate your house. ⁶ Has anyone here just planted a vineyard but not yet eaten any of its fruit? If so, you may go home! You might die in battle, and someone else would eat the first fruit. ⁷ Has anyone here just become engaged to a woman but not yet married her? Well, you may go home and get married! You might die in the battle, and someone else would marry her.'

⁸ "Then the officers will also say, 'Is anyone here afraid or worried? If you are, you may go home before you frighten anyone else.'"

I love the last one. If you are worried, then you might as well just go home! Fear is apparently such a contagious condition that the officers try to prevent it from spreading. We tend to think of worry as a fact of life, something that everyone does to some degree. More and more, I have come to see worry as SIN with a capital "S." Not only does it rob you of peace, but think of what it communicates to those around you. I read somewhere about a dog that was formerly abused and cowered every time its new master approached him. Imagine how our worry reflects how we view our Master.

Read how John MacArthur explains worry:

For some reason, we think of doubt and worry as "small" sins. But when a Christian displays unbelief. . . or an inability to cope with life, he is saying to the world, "My God cannot be trusted," and that kind of disrespect makes one guilty of a fundamental error, the heinous sin of dishonoring God. That is no small sin.37

The Bible has many suggestions for how to deal with worry.

1 Peter 5:6-7

⁶So humble yourselves under the mighty power of God, and at the right time he will lift you up in honor. ⁷Give all your worries and cares to God, for he cares about you.

Other versions say cast your cares, which is the same phrase that is used on Palm Sunday when people throw their coats onto the colt for Jesus to ride. The motion involves setting something down deliberately, and, more importantly, leaving it there.

Matthew 6:25-24

[25] "That is why I tell you not to worry about everyday life—whether you have enough food and drink, or enough clothes to wear. Isn't life more than food, and your body more than clothing? [26] Look at the birds. They don't plant or harvest or store food in barns, for your heavenly Father feeds them. And aren't you far more valuable to him than they are? [27] Can all your worries add a single moment to your life?

[28] "And why worry about your clothing? Look at the lilies of the field and how they grow. They don't work or make their clothing, [29] yet Solomon in all his glory was not dressed as beautifully as they are. [30] And if God cares so wonderfully for wildflowers that are here today and thrown into the fire tomorrow, he will certainly care for you. Why do you have so little faith?

[31] "So don't worry about these things, saying, 'What will we eat? What will we drink? What will we wear?' [32] These things dominate the thoughts of unbelievers, but your heavenly Father already knows all your needs. [33] Seek the Kingdom of God above all else, and live righteously, and he will give you everything you need.

[34] "So don't worry about tomorrow, for tomorrow will bring its own worries. Today's trouble is enough for today.

The word we translate as "worry" is actually a Greek word that means "care." Modern readers tend to read it with gentle, compassionate, positive connotations. It actually means "to be drawn in a different direction." We are drawn away from our loving Father when we worry.

Luke 21:14

Make up your mind right now not to worry about it.

I like the simplicity of this verse. We can control our thoughts to the extent that we can decide not to worry.

Psalm 139:23-24

²³ Search me, O God, and know my heart;
test me and know my anxious thoughts.
²⁴ Point out anything in me that offends you,
and lead me along the path of everlasting life.

Again, this is not that difficult. Ask God to reveal what is bothering you and give it to Him. The following passage may already be in your memory bank. It is often quoted because it contains so much useful information.

Philippians 4:4-9

⁴ Always be full of joy in the Lord. I say it again—rejoice!
⁵ Let everyone see that you are considerate in all you do. Remember, the Lord is coming soon.

⁶ Don't worry about anything; instead, pray about everything. Tell God what you need and thank him for all he has done. ⁷ Then you will experience God's peace, which exceeds anything we can understand. His peace will guard your hearts and minds as you live in Christ Jesus.

⁸ And now, dear brothers and sisters, one final thing. Fix your thoughts on what is true, and honorable, and right, and pure, and lovely, and admirable. Think about things that are excellent and worthy of praise. ⁹ Keep putting into practice all you learned and received from me—everything you heard from me and saw me doing. Then the God of peace will be with you.

Instead of worrying, we are told to focus on positive things.

"True" does not necessarily mean easy. We may have a Scarlett O'Hara syndrome and want to think about it tomorrow. Maybe there's a hard-to-swallow truth about your life that you need to face directly.

"Honorable" involves admitting when we exaggerate or sugar coat something. Be honest in your own thoughts about your motivations, desires, and habits.

"Right" means just and fair. Use the same standards for yourself that you would apply to others.

"Pure" means listening to your conscience.

"Lovely" and "admirable" suggest concentrating on a beautiful experience or a good relationship when you are feeling down. Creation alone can give you lots of material.

Paul again urges us to control our thought life, which includes banishing worry. You may recognize the phrase, "take captive every thought."

2 Corinthians 10:3-5 (NIV)

> [3] For though we live in the world, we do not wage war as the world does. [4] The weapons we fight with are not the weapons of the world. On the contrary, they have divine power to demolish strongholds. [5] We demolish arguments and every pretension that sets itself up against the knowledge of God, and we take captive every thought to make it obedient to Christ.

I just discovered the way The Message phrases the above passage.

> We use our powerful God-tools for smashing warped philosophies, tearing down barriers erected against the truth of God, fitting every loose thought and emotion and impulse into the structure of life shaped by Christ.

Isn't that inspiring? "Fitting every loose thought… into the structure of life shaped by Christ."

So, how do we control our thought life enough to not worry? I think one way is to remember when God speaks. Acts 10:19 says, "While Peter was still thinking about the vision" (NIV), and we know that Jesus' Mom "treasured up all these things and pondered them in her heart" (Luke 2:19 NIV).

I have mentioned this before, and I need to get back into the habit myself, but journaling and note taking are vital. If God tells you something, hold onto it. Bob and I went to a friend's church in Colorado with a prophetic ministry. He received a word from God and the staff wrote it down for him to take so that he would remember it. Years later at our own church, we were encouraged to tape record with our cell phones when someone was speaking. You think you'll remember, but you won't.

Another method is to use your God-given imagination. As an actor, I have an over-stimulated imagination so I particularly like this technique. On the flip side, it can work against me. People with active imaginations can imagine the worst possible scenarios. I think it was Mark Twain who said, "I am an old man and have known a great many troubles, but most of them never happened." Use imagination correctly and picture the invisible and eternal realities. Try thinking of what heaven will be like or focus on Jesus sitting next to you.

Lastly, I think we tend to worry when we don't see answers to our prayers coming quickly enough to fit our timetable. Our minds race: "Is God listening? Doesn't He get how important this is? What's going to happen?" The following Old Testament story is incredibly encouraging to me.

Daniel 10:4-14

4 On April 23, as I was standing on the bank of the great Tigris River, 5 I looked up and saw a man dressed in linen clothing, with a belt of pure gold around his waist. 6 His body looked like a precious gem. His face flashed like lightning, and his eyes flamed like torches. His arms and feet shone like polished bronze, and his voice roared like a vast multitude of people.

7 Only I, Daniel, saw this vision. The men with me saw nothing, but they were suddenly terrified and ran away to hide. 8 So I was left there all alone to see this amazing vision. My strength left me, my face grew deathly pale, and I felt very weak. 9 Then I heard the man speak, and when I heard the sound of his voice, I fainted and lay there with my face to the ground.

10 Just then a hand touched me and lifted me, still trembling, to my hands and knees. 11 And the man said to me, "Daniel, you are very precious to God, so listen carefully to what I have to say to you. Stand up, for I have been sent to you." When he said this to me, I stood up, still trembling.

12 Then he said, "Don't be afraid, Daniel. Since the first day you began to pray for understanding and to humble yourself before your God, your request has been heard in heaven. I

have come in answer to your prayer. [13] But for twenty-one days the spirit prince of the kingdom of Persia blocked my way. Then Michael, one of the archangels, came to help me, and I left him there with the spirit prince of the kingdom of Persia. [14] Now I am here to explain what will happen to your people in the future, for this vision concerns a time yet to come."

Did you catch it? "Since the first day you began to pray" God heard and began to act. There are things happening in the spiritual world that we will never understand. Our job is not to figure out why but to trust in the Almighty Creator of the Universe who has already sent an "answer to your prayer."

> Let worry or anxiety be like an alarm clock in your walk with God. When you start to worry, let that wake you up to prayer. Wake up spiritually and mentally and then lift up the matter to the Lord in prayer. It will make a difference in your worry and your walk.[38]

Bob's accident happened over 30 years ago, and he has prayed many, many times for pain relief and for deliverance from his wheelchair. Almost two years ago, he tried a new, holistic supplement, and the worst of his pain disappeared overnight. He was amazed and incredibly grateful.

Little did we know, God wasn't done yet. Bob's neurologist ordered an MRI to check on the condition of his spine. He is an incomplete quadriplegic. She warned us that his back was most likely deteriorating because he sits all day and is getting older. We would be lucky if it stayed the same. When he met with her again, she was crying. His spine had improved! Bob now has the back of a healthy 60-year old. His nerves are actually returning to life.

My faith is incredibly strengthened by this report. Never ever give up on God. We don't understand His timing, but He is to be trusted. Kick worry out the door and praise your Savior.

POINTS TO PONDER:

Take a few moments and think about the quote below. Jot down some responses.

"When Satan spins molehills into mountains, when he convinces us we're all alone, when he hammers at our deficiencies, when he recounts our inadequacies...

Worried saints back away from their duty, bury their talents and lose their blessings. They miss the destiny God planned for them."[39]

Lord Jesus, I know that I am not alone. I not only have You, but I know that _____ loves me and is praying for me.

Sometimes I still believe the devil's lie that I am: _____
_____

Help me to remember that I have a talent in the area of: _____
_____

PRAYER:

Jesus, I confess that worry enters my mind. Next time that I want to dwell on an unknown future, remind me that You love me and have me in Your hands.

38
I WILL MAKE YOU MY WIFE FOREVER

"Never love anybody who treats
you like you're ordinary."

– OSCAR WILDE

I wish that I had a dollar for every time a well-meaning (married) friend would tell me, "God isn't going to send you a husband until you are happy without one." I understand the theory behind this statement. After all, the apostle Paul said to be content in every situation. But, somehow, it got twisted in my head to mean that I wasn't allowed to want to be married. Have you ever felt like saying back to those women, "easy for you to say, sitting at home with a wonderful family!"?

I left this chapter for last even though it may be the one you wanted to read first. If you haven't spent time developing your walk with the Lord Jesus, then nothing in this section will help because, ultimately, it is His plan for you to be single *right now.*

> God crucified Jesus; God made Sara barren; God afflicted Job; God sent Moses to the desert for 40 years; God orchestrated David's wilderness wanderings; God took Naomi's husband and two sons. When God does something to you, all you can do is submit and pray and wait for God to fulfil His purposes...

> You've been persevering for weeks, or months, or possibly even years. You've known darkness, pain, perplexity and fire. You don't understand why God is allowing all his. And then one day it's as though you awaken from a sleep, and it suddenly hits you: "I'm different! God has used this trial to revolutionize me. This tribulation is none other than the love of God for me."

> Character produces hope because when I see God working in my life and changing me, I know that He's not going to do a half-baked job. What God starts He finishes.[40]

Looking back now, I truly believe that those longings I felt to have a husband were God-given. He invented marriage. The desire I had was legitimate. The challenge was to accept God's answer. Turning into a whining and bitter woman was not going to get me very far.

Proverbs 30:21-23

> There are three things that make the earth tremble—no, four it cannot endure: a slave who becomes king, an overbearing fool who prospers, a bitter woman who finally gets a husband, a servant girl who supplants her mistress.

First of all, how does God feel about you as His bride?

I told the little girl that stays with us on the weekend that sometimes I cry when she leaves on Sundays because I miss her. Her nickname for herself is Mae Mae. She started telling me "Mae Mae come back" when she was picked up and headed out with her guardian. During a women's Bible study at my home, I told the group a story about my grandson's funeral and got tears in my eyes. Our little one climbed up on my lap, a little astonished, and said, "Nana! Mae Mae *here*. Mae Mae *home*. No cry!"

Don't you think our bridegroom wants to tell you the same thing? I am *here*. I love you.

Zephaniah 3:17 (NIV)

The Lord your God is with you,
 the Mighty Warrior who saves.
 He will take great delight in you;
 in his love he will no longer rebuke you,
 but will rejoice over you with singing.

Israel had a long history of being unfaithful to God. Even so, He continued to reach out in love, and He does so to you today.

Isaiah 54:4-8

[4] "Fear not, for you will not be ashamed. Do not be troubled, for you will not be put to shame. You will forget how you were ashamed when you were young. You will not remember the sorrow of being without a husband any more. [5] Your Maker is your husband. His name is the Lord of All. And the One Who saves you is the Holy One of Israel. He is called the God of All the earth. [6] For the Lord has called you like a wife left alone and filled with sorrow, like a wife who married when young and is left," says your God. [7] "For a short time I left you, but with much loving-pity I will take you back. [8] When I was very angry I hid My face from you for a short time. But with loving-kindness that lasts forever I will have pity on you," says the Lord Who bought you and saves you.

There's a promise, too, for those who think they don't deserve God's love anymore. The entire book of Hosea is dedicated to those who have strayed sexually and are embarrassed to return to His offer of marriage.

Hosea 2:14-16, 19-20

> But then I will win her back once again.
> I will lead her into the desert
> and speak tenderly to her there.
> I will return her vineyards to her
> and transform the Valley of Trouble into a gateway of hope.
> She will give herself to me there,
> as she did long ago when she was young,
> when I freed her from her captivity in Egypt.
> When that day comes," says the LORD,
> "you will call me 'my husband'
> instead of 'my master.'
> I will make you my wife forever,
> showing you righteousness and justice,
> unfailing love and compassion.
> [20] I will be faithful to you and make you mine,
> and you will finally know me as the Lord."

How does this work in real life? Jeremiah 31:32 says that God "loved (Israel) like a husband loves his wife." How does God behave like a husband to the single woman? I'll share one funny example with you. When I was a missionary in Chicago, I moved into a new apartment. The refrigerator was delivered and left on the back step. I managed to coax it into the tiny alcove where it was meant to fit, and then it got stuck. The only bathroom was behind it, so I had to climb up and over the fridge to get to it. I pushed and pulled in vain. It was truly wedged. After a bout of tears and self-pity, I sat on top of the fridge and prayed. It went something like this: "Okay, God, Your word promises that You will be my husband. Well, right now, I need a husband to move this fridge, and You're it!" It was nothing more spiritual than that, I promise you. Well, you guessed it. I got down, gave the appliance a little push, and it slid in like it was covered in butter. I wish I had a selfie of the happy dance I did on my kitchen floor!

More than a decade after being married, I gained more insight into the reality of Jesus as a husband to those who are single. We attended a wedding, and as I was listening to the new couple recite their vows, I imagined it was Jesus and me standing at the altar. He was holding my hands and looking at me with eyes brimming with adoration. He said, "I promise to love you, comfort you, honor and keep you for better or worse, for richer or poorer, in sickness and health." That vision gave me goosebumps!

Looking Elsewhere

Remember the love story of Jacob and Rachel? Jacob fell in love with Rachel at first sight, but her father insisted that Jacob first marry the older sister, Leah. Jacob did so only in order to gain Rachel's hand.

> Genesis 29:31-35
>
> "When the Lord saw that Leah was unloved, he enabled her to have children, but Rachel could not conceive. So Leah became pregnant and gave birth to a son. She named him Reuben, for she said, 'The Lord has noticed my misery, and now my husband will love me.' She soon became pregnant again and gave birth to another son. She named him Simeon, for she said, 'The Lord heard that I was unloved and has given me another son.' Then she became pregnant a third time and gave birth to another son. She named him Levi, for she said, 'Surely this time my husband will feel affection for me, since I have given him three sons!' Once again Leah became pregnant and gave birth to another son. She named him Judah, for she said, 'Now I will praise the Lord!' And then she stopped having children."

Can you relate to Leah's attitude? What things have you tried to do in order to gain affection from a man? What is Leah's ultimate conclusion?

For me, the moral of this story is that even marriage does not guarantee happiness. This may be a truism, but it's one many single women nod assent to but don't really believe. When I was in my 20s and 30s, I had a series of girlfriends that gave up on finding a Christian husband and went looking elsewhere like bars and online dating services. Every one of them ended up divorced or abused or unhappy. That is **not** to say that all nonbelievers make terrible husbands. But I do believe that when women choose to disobey God with their eyes wide open, they also must be prepared for the consequences.

Throughout the years, I have kept many journals and often lamented my singleness in them. It all comes down to trust. Here's a quote from when I was 40:

> Do I believe God has a purpose for my life? Can I trust Him to bring me what I need emotionally and relationally? If it would serve Him for me to be married, He is capable of putting someone in my path. If I cannot only be more useful to Him but truly happier single—for He desires me to live joyfully—can I walk confidently towards that future?

So, if you are single and waiting, the struggle is to find that balance (that word again!) between faith that He does answer prayers and contentment while you wait.

POINTS TO PONDER:

From the verses quoted in this chapter, God declares that He:

> Takes great delight in you
> Rejoices over you with singing
> Has loving-kindness for you that lasts forever
> Will be faithful to you and make you His
> Notices your misery

Write down a response to what your Husband is offering.

_____

_____

PRAYER:

Help me understand the many ways You want to show Your love to me. Thank You for being not just my friend but for feeling crazy, passionate, sacrificial love for me.

Bibliography

[1] Paraphrased from a sermon by Pastor Mark Jobe, New Life Church, Chicago, IL.

[2] Henry T. Blackaby & Charles V. King, *Experiencing God*, Broadman & Holman Publishers, p. 148.

[3] Madeline L'Engle, *The Weather of the Heart,* Harold Shaw Publishers, 1978, p. 50.

[4] Hannah Hurnard, *Hinds Feet on High Places,* Living Books, 1975, pp.82, 83

[5] C.S. Lewis, *The Problem of Pain*, HarperOne, 1940.

[6] R.C. Sproul, *The Intimate Marriage*, P&R Publishing, 1975, pp. 127-128.

[7] C.S. Lewis, *The Weight of Glory and Other Addresses,* MacMillan Publishing Company, 1949.

[8] Henry T. Blackaby & Claude V. King, *Experiencing God,* Broadman & Holman Publishers, 1998, p. 220.

[9] Paraphrased from a sermon by Gary Jones, First Assembly of God Church, San Diego, CA on November 12, 1995.

[10] Ibid.

[11] Richard J. Foster, *Celebration of Discipline,* Harper & Row Publishers, 1978, p 33.

[12] C.S. Lewis, *Mere Christianity,* Harper Collins Publishers, 1952, p. 168.

[13] Philip Yancey, *What's So Amazing About Grace?*, Zondervan Publishing House, 1997, p. 143.

[14] Anthony Bloom, *Beginning to Pray,* Paulist Press, 1970, p. 5.

[15] Philip Yancy, *Prayer*, Zondervan, 2006, p. 166.

[16] Anthony Bloom, *Beginning to Pray*, Paulist Press, 1970, p. 101.

[17] *McCabe:* Herbert McCabe, *God, Christ and Us* (London: Continuum International Publishing Group, 2005). Quoted in L. Roger Owens "Don't Talk Nonsense," *Christian Century* (January 25, 2005), p. 21. Quoted in Philip Yancy, Prayer, Zondervan, 2006, p. 187

[18] Henry T. Blackaby & Claude V. King, *Experiencing God*, Broadman & Holman Publishers, 1998, p. 228.

[19] Bob Sorge, *The Fire of Delayed Answers,* Oasis House, 1996. p. 42.

[20] Alvin J. Vander Griend, "Your Prayers Matter," *Discipleship Journal*, 1999, Issue 111.

[21] Philip Yancy, *Prayer,* Zondervan, 2006, p. 303.

[22] Henry T. Blackaby & Claude V. King, *Experiencing God*, Broadman & Holman Publishers, 1998, pp. 180-181

[23] Borrowed from a sermon I heard by Bill Wilson "Metro World Child Ministries"). Bill worked with street kids and had been tempted to give up many times. One day he did give up. He was mugged, and his face was bashed in with a brick, blinding him in one eye. He secretly bought a plane ticket and was going to disappear the next morning because he'd had enough. But when he woke up and opened his eyes, he could see! God had healed him overnight.

[24] Jerry Bridges, *The Pursuit of Holiness*, NavPress, 1996, p. 102.

[25] Paraphrased from a sermon by Pastor Alex Rowland, First Assembly of God Church, San Diego. (Now City View Church).

[26] Hannah Hurnard, *Hinds Feet on High Places,* Living Books, 1975 pp. 172-173.

[27] C.S. Lewis, *Mere Christianity,* Harper Collins Publishers, 1952.

[28] Charles Hummel, *Freedom From Tyranny of the Urgent,* Inter-Varsity Christian Fellowship of the United States of America, 1994, p.10.

[29] Philip Yancy, *Prayer,* Zondervan, 2006, p. 31.

[30] *Nouwen:* Henri Nouwen, *With Open Hands* (New York: Ballantine/Epiphany Edition, 1985), 54. Quoted in Philip Yancy, *Prayer,* Zondervan, 2006, p. 34.

[31] Bruce Wilkinson, *The Prayer of Jabez,* Multnomah Publishers, Inc., 2000.

[32] Joyce Meyers, *Battlefield of the Mind:* Winning the Battlefield in Your Mind, Warner Books Edition, 1995.

[33] Ibid.

[34] Philip Yancey, *"What's So Amazing About Grace?"* Zondervan Publishing House, 1997, p. 41.

[35] Ibid., pg. 60.

[36] Henry T. Blackaby & Claude V. King, *Experiencing God,* Broadman & Holman Publishers, 1998, p. 30.

[37] John MacArthur, *The Ultimate Priority,* Moody Press, 1983, p. 140.

[38] Rick Shepherd, *Praying God's Way,* AMG Publishers, 2003, pg. 139.

[39] Carey Lewis, former director of now-defunct Actors, Models and Talent for Christ, from on-line devotion *"Gotcha's Demons: Worry, Fear & Cowardice."*

[40] Bob Sorge, *The Fire of Delayed Answers,* Oasis House, 1996. p. 42.

Appendix

My Story

I grew up assuming I was a Christian. My parents had been raised in a strict, legalistic church in Missouri which drove Dad away from the Lord completely and caused Mom years of searching for a personal God. We went to church every Sunday, but we moved every two years so I got a sampling of Baptist, Church of England, Episcopalian, and Presbyterian churches.

We moved to California my senior year in high school. For the first time, I met Christians my age who were vocal about their faith and took pains to make sure I knew what I was missing. I finally had a personal encounter with God on March 29, 1975. (See more of that story in chapter 24.)

That knowledge of His love never left me, although I didn't always walk in step with Him. My freshman year of college, I walked a tightrope between the Bible studies and church activities I was involved in and the group of secular friends with whom I spent the majority of my time. We hung out and messed around, and I became crude and careless in my speech and thoughts. I continued my quiet times and was even used by God occasionally, but I had a lot to learn about making Jesus Lord over all the areas of my life.

Transferring to a Christian college (Point Loma Nazarene, San Diego) my sophomore year took me out of the bad habits I was starting to develop and gave me a chance to grow up in the Word. At times, however, this new school was almost more difficult because it was so much easier to slide when everyone around you assumes you are a Christian. I attended Bible studies and really tried to seek God's face but always had the feeling He required more of me. My junior year, I was a Resident Assistant in my dorm. Just being in a leadership position made me want to get my own life together. What I said to the girls had less of an effect than how I carried this advice out in my own walk. I had moments of rebellion against having to live up to these standards until I realized that it was God setting these codes of behavior, not the administration.

My senior year, God became supremely real to me. My prayer life changed tremendously as I saw His grace bestowed again and again. I stopped being afraid of claiming His power in situations and asking for specific needs to be met. It was at this time that I came to First Assembly of God, San Diego (now City View Church) where I stayed for decades.

I interned twice and helped write a book on how to lead small groups. I often taught the singles' class (Mainpoint) plus dozens of Bible studies. I helped the team in planning events, retreats, car rallies, camping trips, etc. I lived in San Diego for 20 years.

In 1996 after receiving my Master's degree in Theology, I moved to Chicago to be a missionary. I was recruited by an inner-city church to develop Bible studies. I thought it would be a slam dunk assignment. After all, I was a seminary graduate and had facilitated plenty of small groups. I was intensely humbled. My rich white church on the hill in San Diego did not prepare me for the mostly Mexican, working class, Catholic women in my neighborhood. New Life pastored by Mark Jobe is an incredible church with many church plants. I learned a great deal—mostly I learned that I didn't know anything!

Later, I ended up moving to Hudson, WI because my dad lived there. Thank goodness I moved because that's where I met Bob. I didn't get married until I was 46. My prayers sounded something like this:

Now I lay me down to sleep,
I pray for a man who's not a creep.

One who's handsome, smart and strong,
Who's not afraid to admit when he is wrong.

One who thinks before he speaks.

When he promises to call, he doesn't wait six weeks.

I pray that he is gainfully employed,
Won't lose his cool when he's annoyed.

Pulls out my chair and opens my door,
Massages my back and begs to do more.

Oh, send me a man who will make love to my mind.
Know what to say when I ask, "How fat is my behind?"

One who'll make love till my body's a' itchin'
He brings ME a sandwich too, when he goes to the kitchen.

I pray that this man will love me to no end,
And never compare me to my best friend.
Thank you in advance, and now I'll just wait,
For I know you will send him before it's too late.

Amen (Author unknown)

I was scared to get engaged. In 1987, Bob had had a horrible work accident that caused him to be an incomplete quadriplegic. I was nervous about marrying someone who used a wheelchair, but I trusted that he was the right man for my life. Bob had been married twice before. His first wife died of leukemia and left him with three small children shortly after his accident. He raised his children for a number of years before getting married again to a woman who had her own daughter. That lady had an affair and divorced him, leaving her teen for him to raise.

Bob and I have grown to love and respect each other tremendously. Being a kind of caregiver is challenging for me, and we don't get the sunset walks on the beach that other couples enjoy, but I wouldn't trade him for anyone. He has a passion for music and sang at nursing homes several times a week for years. He manages a Nashville recording artist, and he even has some songs on the radio himself.

I always thought that maybe God didn't hear my prayers about being a wife and mom since it took me so long in life to find the right man. But Bob's four grown children have given me nine grandkids, and I adore being Nana to them. I figured that was the Lord's answer to all those decades of praying to be a mom.

Then, in 2015 we took in a 19-year-old pregnant girl who had no place to live. She stayed with us for five months. It's a long story, but we ended up helping to raise her little girl three to four days a week. I have enjoyed every moment of being a part-time mommy in every sense of the word. God had a plan all those years I thought He was ignoring me.

I pray that you can take hope in my story. God is not finished with you!

My Father's Voice

I called my dad today just to hear his voice
Though he's far away, I felt at home
As I said goodbye I began to cry
'cause I love my father's voice

My father's voice is so sweet to me
I feel his love and know we're family
I know in my heart he'll never stop loving me
Forever child, forever dad

I remember stories that my daddy told
Bedtime tales just for me
Snuggling close to keep away the cold
Precious memories often told

People say that I look a lot like him
But it's his voice I wish I had
Deep and calm with a soothing touch
Sounds I miss and love so much

His love shines true to me,
Words ring strong but calm
Kindness there righting wrong
I wish all could see
How he loves so free and
what he means to me, my dad

I have a heavenly Father, you know
And when He calls to me, will I go?

Do I love His voice like my other dad?
And will I serve Him or just say no?

Both my Fathers' voices I know so well
They have guided me night and day
Giving hope and peace when I turn my head
Ignoring the words, the words they say

Will you listen when your Father calls?
Let Him pick you up when you fall?
Will you just let go and make the choice?
And just listen to your Father's voice

CPSIA information can be obtained
at www.ICGtesting.com
Printed in the USA
FFHW012349030419
51495155-56949FF